Thomas Kelly Cheyne

Jewish Religious Life after the Exile

Thomas Kelly Cheyne

Jewish Religious Life after the Exile

ISBN/EAN: 9783743340107

Manufactured in Europe, USA, Canada, Australia, Japa

Cover: Foto ©ninafisch / pixelio.de

Manufactured and distributed by brebook publishing software (www.brebook.com)

Thomas Kelly Cheyne

Jewish Religious Life after the Exile

*AMERICAN LECTURES ON THE
HISTORY OF RELIGIONS*

THIRD SERIES—1897-1898

JEWISH RELIGIOUS LIFE AFTER THE EXILE

BY

THE REV. T. K. CHEYNE, M.A., D.D.

Oriel Professor of the Interpretation of Holy Scripture at Oxford,
and formerly Fellow of Balliol College;
Canon of Rochester

G. P. PUTNAM'S SONS
NEW YORK AND LONDON
The Knickerbocker Press
1898

ANNOUNCEMENT.

THE American Lectures on the History of Religions are delivered under the auspices of the American Committee for Lectures on the History of Religions. This Committee was organised in 1892 for the purpose of instituting "popular courses in the History of Religions, somewhat after the style of the Hibbert lectures in England, to be delivered annually by the best scholars of Europe and this country, in various cities, such as Baltimore, Boston, Brooklyn, Chicago, New York, Philadelphia, and others."

The terms of association under which the Committee exists are as follows:

1.—The object of this Association shall be to provide courses of lectures on the history of religions, to be delivered in various cities.
2.—The Association shall be composed of delegates from Institutions agreeing to co-operate, or from Local Boards, organised where such co-operation is not possible.
3.—These delegates—one from each Institution or Local Board—shall constitute themselves a

Council under the name of the "American Committee for Lectures on the History of Religions."

4.—The Council shall elect out of its number a President, a Secretary, and a Treasurer.

5.—All matters of local detail shall be left to the Institutions or Local Boards, under whose auspices the lectures are to be delivered.

6.—A course of lectures on some religion, or phase of religion, from an historical point of view, or on a subject germane to the study of religions, shall be delivered annually, or at such intervals as may be found practicable, in the different cities represented by this Association.

7.—The Council (*a*) shall be charged with the selection of the lecturers, (*b*) shall have charge of the funds, (*c*) shall assign the time for the lectures in each city, and perform such other functions as may be necessary.

8.—Polemical subjects, as well as polemics in the treatment of subjects, shall be positively excluded.

9.—The lecturer shall be chosen by the Council at least ten months before the date fixed for the course of lectures.

10.—The lectures shall be delivered in the various cities between the months of October and June.

Announcement

11.—The copyright of the lectures shall be the property of the Association.

12.—One half of the lecturer's compensation shall be paid at the completion of the entire course, and the second half upon the publication of the lectures.

13.—The compensation offered to the lecturer shall be fixed in each case by the Council.

14.—The lecturer is not to deliver elsewhere any of the lectures for which he is engaged by the Committee, except with the sanction of the Committee.

The Committee as now constituted is as follows:
C. H. Toy (Harvard University), Chairman.
Morris Jastrow, Jr. (University of Pa.), Secretary.
John P. Peters (New York), Treasurer.
Francis Brown (Union Theological Seminary).
Richard J. H. Gottheil (Columbia University).
Paul Haupt (Johns Hopkins University).
Franklin W. Hooper (Brooklyn Institute).
J. F. Jameson (Brown University).
George F. Moore (Andover Theological Seminary).
F. K. Sanders (Yale University).
J. G. Schurman (Cornell University).

The first course of American Lectures on the History of Religions was delivered in the winter of

1894-1895, by Prof. T. W. Rhys-Davids, Ph.D., LL.D., of London, England. His subject was the History and Literature of Buddhism. The second course was delivered in 1896-1897, by Prof. Daniel G. Brinton, A.M., M.D., LL.D., Sc.D., of Philadelphia, on the Religions of Primitive Peoples. These lectures were published in book form by Messrs. G. P. Putnam's Sons, publishers to the Committee, under the above titles, in 1896 and 1897 respectively.

The third course of lectures was delivered in 1897-1898, on Jewish Religious Life after the Exile, by the Rev. T. K. Cheyne, M.A., D.D., Oriel Professor of the Interpretation of Holy Scriptures at Oxford, and Canon of Rochester, and is contained in the present volume, the third of the series. These lectures were delivered at the following places:

Andover (Andover Theological Seminary).
Baltimore (Johns Hopkins University).
Boston (Lowell Institute).
Brooklyn (Brooklyn Institute).
Ithaca (Cornell University).
New Haven (Yale University).
New York (Union Theological Seminary).
Philadelphia (University of Pennsylvania).
Providence (Brown University Lecture Association).

Professor Cheyne is one of the leading Biblical

Announcement

scholars of the day, whose contributions to the critical study of the Old Testament have profoundly influenced both scholars and laymen, and needs no introduction to the public. His most important publications are the following: *The Prophecies of Isaiah, Job and Solomon, The Book of Psalms, The Origin and Religious Contents of the Psalter* (Bampton Lectures, 1889), *The Hallowing of Criticism, Jeremiah and his Times, Introduction to the Book of Isaiah*, and a new critical edition of the text of Isaiah with a translation and commentary, in the *Polychrome Bible*.

The American Lectures on the History of Religions for 1898-1899 will be delivered by Prof. Karl Budde, Ph.D., of Strasburg, on the theme, Religious Life and Thought among the Hebrews in Pre-Exilic Days. The lecturer for 1899-1900 will be Edouard Naville, of Geneva, the well-known Egyptologist.

JOHN P. PETERS,
C. H. TOY,
MORRIS JASTROW, JR.,
} *Committee on Publication.*

MAY, 1898.

CONTENTS.

LECTURE I. RELIGIOUS LIFE IN JUDÆA BEFORE THE ARRIVAL OF NEHEMIAH.

PAGE

The Judæan population before Ezra's time—Inquiry into the tone of their religion—Haggai and Zechariah—Completion of the second temple—The true commencement of the post-exilic period—Zerubbabel put forward as Messianic king—Attitude of Zechariah towards fasting—His theological explanation of Israel's calamity—His deficiencies as a moralist made good by "Malachi"—Spiritual improvement in the Jerusalem community; appearance of a band of strict observers of Deuteronomy—Prophetic record of an attempt, before that of Ezra, to stir up the Babylonian Jews—Contrast between Ezekiel and Isa. xlix.-lv.—The former more influential at Jerusalem than the latter—Fresh light on the relations between the Jews and the Samaritans, and between the orthodox and the heretical Jews—Nehemiah's violent conduct towards the Samaritans; its explanation—Survey of results—The Jewish priest Manasseh; his services to the Samaritans—Jews and Samaritans compared—Their unconscious agreement as to the essence of religion—Attitude of Jesus to the Jewish law and to individual Samaritans . . 1–35

LECTURE II. NEHEMIAH, EZRA, AND MANASSEH; OR, THE RECONSTITUTION OF THE JEWISH AND THE SAMARITAN COMMUNITIES.

The exiles in Babylonia not deficient in patriotism—Their literary occupations directed to practical objects—Object of the first appendix to the Second Isaiah (chaps. xlix.-lv.)—More directly practical spirit of the Jews who visited Nehemiah, a butler of Artaxerxes Longimanus (?)—Nehemiah's character and work—His statements not to be accepted without criticism. Quite probable that Jewish prophets had represented Nehemiah as the Messiah—Sanballat at first sincerely desired a compromise—Nehemiah probably departed when the wall was ready—He must have been missed ; in fact, his work was but half done—The Samaritan connection was not broken off—Object of Ezra and his companions —The formation of the congregation—Reappearance of Nehemiah as governor or high commissioner—His three practical objects—Ezra's law-book—In what sense it can be called new—Its object, the holiness of the community—Law of the Day of Atonement ; its strange details—Ezra's book not exclusively legal—Religious character of the narratives of the introduction—The new ideals of the " humble ones " in the lives of the patriarchs, rewritten in the Priestly Code, also partly in the life of Job—Sanctification must precede deliverance ; hence a minute code was necessary . 36–81

LECTURE III. JEWISH RELIGIOUS IDEALS; HINDRANCES TO THEIR PERFECT DEVELOPMENT.

Troubles of the Jews in the post-exilic period—A religious compensation, viz., the increased prominence of the Israelitish ideal as a subject of meditation—Evidence of this : (1) A cycle of four songs on the " Servant of Jehovah " inserted in, and interwoven with, Isa. xl.-lv.—In Isa. lii., 13–liii., 12, the " Servant " is a fusion of all martyrs and confessors; in xlii., 1-4, xlix., 1-6, l., 4-9, not of all, but of those only who preached and expounded the religious law—(2) Prophecies of the Messianic king—Early history of this form of belief— (3) Psalms of the " Messianic king " or " Royal psalms "— Sternness of the foreign policy ascribed to the Messiah— Accuracy of the psalmist's descriptions wrongly denied— Heathen oppressors—Division of the Jews into the wicked rich and the righteous poor not an exhaustive classification —The latter are but the inner circle of Israel ; around them are the great mass of less perfect Israelites, who need the guidance of wiser men than themselves . . . 82–125

Contents   xi

LECTURE IV. JEWISH WISDOM; ITS MEANING, OBJECT, AND VARIETIES.

PAGE

Recognition of the necessity of systematic instruction of the young—Mythical founder of the "Wisdom-Literature"— One of the chief prerequisites of wisdom, loving-kindness— The want of this makes a man a " fool "—And wide as is the influence of the wise, it does not extend to the " fool "— Wisdom and prosperity go together—Religious aspect of wisdom—Proverbs, like the Law, presupposes the theory of earthly retribution—Difficulty of the Proverbs respecting the king —No systematic Messianic element exists in Ecclesiasticus or Proverbs—A less severely practical view of wisdom (Prov. viii., 22-31 ; Job xxviii., 1-27 ; xxxviii., xxxix.)—If the first part of wisdom is the fear of Jehovah, its latter part has a wider range—The inquisitive spirit finely expressed in the speeches of Jehovah—Wisdom moderates the divine power—She is herself powerful beyond expression ; it is a pastime to her to elaborate a world—Affinities of these strange new ideas— The personification of wisdom ; Egyptian and especially Persian (Zoroastrian) parallels ; Greek parallels less appropriate— The true Book of Job—The suggestiveness of the story only discovered after the Exile—The original book reconstructed ; its influence on Isa. liii. ; parallelism of the two works— Considerations which led to the insertion of the dialogues— Change in the conception of Job's character—The writer refuted (as he must have thought) the old doctrine of unfailing retribution—But he did not solve the problem of suffering   126-172

LECTURE V. ORTHODOX AND HERETICAL WISDOM ; CONTEMPORARY LEVITICAL PIETY.

The spirit of doubt enters Judaism from Greece—A record of this in Prov. xxx., 1-4—The author, a Hellenising Jew, a prototype of Goethe's Faust—Orthodox protest in Prov. xxx., 5-9 —Evidence that there were other sceptical writings besides Agur's poem—Chief among these is Ecclesiastes—Difficulties of the book—How much religion had the author ?—He is no atheist, but his God is too transcendental—He has also abandoned the belief in God's retributive justice—Such statements as Eccles. vii., 15 ; viii., 14, pained devout readers—Hence references to a present and a future judgment of the wicked were interpolated—Unfortunate consequence of this heterodoxy—God remained, but he could only fear God, not trust Him—Yet his morality is not the lowest: he recommends the pleasures of the table, but with a sad irony—His social sense is weak, and his Jewish feeling almost extinct—Opinions divided about Ecclesiastes—Since they could not suppress the book, the authorities determined to mitigate its heterodoxy and to suggest the idea that the speaker is a *blasé* and penitent king—Addition to the Epilogue—Date of the book : the first possible periods are those of John Hyrcanus (135-105) and Alexander Jannæus (104-78)—Objections to these—The reign of Herod, however, gives the key to the book—The author a philosophic Sadducee—Strong contrast offered by Ben Sira and the Chronicler—The former is more legal in his religion than the earlier moralists ; also more eschatological—The latter is a Levite, and takes a special interest in some of the functions of his class—His belief in present retribution ; interest in prophets ; warm piety 173-215

LECTURE VI   JUDAISM : ITS POWER OF ATTRACTING FOREIGNERS; ITS HIGHER THEOLOGY; ITS RELATION TO GREECE, PERSIA, AND BABYLON.

Contrast between the missionary ideal of the "Servant" songs and the bitter expressions toward foreigners in the psalms of the late Persian period—Two classes of persons among the "nations"—Both alike are "forgetful of God," but the one longs to be better instructed, the other breathes out threatenings against God's people—The ideal of the author of the "Servant" songs was also that of the writer of Jonah—Its more practicable object, to smooth the way for the admission of proselytes at Jerusalem (Isaiah lvi., 1-5)—Book of Ruth—Circumstances favourable to an influx of foreigners be-

PAGE

fore the Greek period—Motives of proselytes various—Hope
of a life after death for the righteous—The poetical books
show that many of the most religious and cultured persons
held out against the new belief—Even the Psalter, which we
might expect to find more hospitable to new beliefs, contains
no reference to Immortality or the Resurrection—Down to
Simon the Maccabee, Resurrection and Immortality not beliefs of the majority—Impressive services of the temple,
helpful to religion—Superstitious formalism; how the
best teachers guarded against it—Ps. xxvi., 5–7; Ps. xv.;
xxiv., 1–6—"Guests of Jehovah" in a new sense—Lib-
eralising effect of the Dispersion—Conceptions of a spiritual
temple and spiritual sacrifices—Prayer and praise, the true
sacrifices; to which add the study of the Law—Growth of
veneration for the Law—Reaction against Hellenism—Jewish religion always susceptible to influences from without—
Babylonia, Persia, Greece; their several contributions to
Judaism—The Zoroastrian hymns compared with the Psalms
—Connection of these inquiries with a much larger one: the
origin and nature of essential Christianity and Judaism 216–261

INDEX 263

INDEX TO BIBLICAL PASSAGES 266

NOTE ON THE DATES OF THE LITERATURE REFERRED TO.

FOR the convenience of the reader a conspectus is here given of the dates of ancient writings referred to.

Haggai and *Zechariah.* Haggai, Sept.–Dec., 520 B.C., Zech. i., 1–6, 520; i., 7–vi., 15, 519; vii., viii., 518.

Lamentations. Lam. i., ii., iv., v., in their present form from the latter part of the Persian period, but probably based on earlier elegies.

Isaiah i.–xxxix., Micah, etc. Messianic passages of post-Exilic origin. Pre-Exilic passages, possibly Jer. xxiii., 5, 6 (xxxiii., 15, 16), and Exilic, certainly Ezek. xvii., 22–24, xxxiv., 23 *f.*, xxxvii., 24 *f.*

Isaiah xl.–lxvi. Isa. xl.–xlviii. (mostly), the original Prophecy of the prophetic writer, commonly, but not very suitably, named the Second Isaiah. Written soon after 546 (?), the year in which Cyrus left Sardis. Chaps. xlix.–lv., an appendix to the preceding prophecy, written (like Chaps. xl.–xlviii.) in Babylonia, but with an eye to the circumstances of Jerusalem. The cycle of poems on the Servant of Jehovah (xlii., 1-4; xlix., 1-6; l., 4-9; lii., 13-liii., 12) probably had at first an independent existence, but was subsequently incorporated by an early writer into the expanded Prophecy of Restoration (*i. e.*, Chaps. xl.-lv.). Chaps. lvi.-lxvi. do not indeed form a single work with a unity of its own, but (with the probable exception of lxiii., 7-lxiv., 12, which is of still later date) all belong to different parts of the age of Nehemiah and Ezra.

Malachi. Shortly before the arrival of Nehemiah (445 ?).

Genesis–Joshua. Priestly Code, provisionally completed by Ezra and his fellows in the first half of the 5th century.

Ezra. The documents in Ezr. v., vi., based upon genuine official records. Ezr. vii., 27-viii., 34 is taken from the Memoirs of Ezra (5th cent.).

Nehemiah. Neh. i., 1-vii., 5, xiii., 6-31, belong to the Memoirs of Nehemiah (5th cent.).

Ruth and *Jonah.* Not long after Nehemiah and Ezra.

Psalms. The hymn-book of the orthodox community founded by Ezra, partly of the late Persian, partly of the Greek period.

Job. A composite work of the late Persian or (more probably) early Greek period.

Proverbs. A composite work of the Persian and Greek periods.

Chronicles (including *Ezra* and *Nehemiah* in their present form). About 250.

Note on the Dates of Literature

Daniel. Age of Antiochus Epiphanes.
Ecclesiastes. Not improbably of the age of Herod the Great. Further research necessary.
Enoch. Composite; 2d and 1st centuries B.C.
Psalms of Solomon. Between 63 and 45. B.C.
For further details see Driver's *Introduction to the Old Testament Literature*, an excellent work, with abundance of facts, but often not sufficiently keen in its criticism; and compare the *Polychrome Bible*, edited by Haupt, and the *Encyclopædia Biblica: A Dictionary of the Bible* (A. & C. Black, London).

NOTE ON PAGE 152.

For a new translation of Job xxxviii., 29–34, by the present writer, see *Journal of Biblical Literature* (Boston, U. S. A.), 1898. The names of constellations are perhaps more correctly given.

PREFACE.

THE aim of the writer has been twofold: 1, to interest the public at large in the history of our mother-religion, the Jewish; and 2, to give students of the post-Exilic period a synthesis of the best critical results at present attainable, and so to enable them to judge of their degree of probability. Perhaps the peculiarity of this volume consists in its union of these two objects. It is possible to be a successful populariser without being an original investigator, and to be an investigator without being a specially interesting writer. How far the author has realised his intentions, it is for others to determine. He has at any rate desired to follow the advice of a French Orientalist,* " not to content ourselves with ten learned readers when we can assemble in our audience all those whom the past of the human spirit charms and attracts."

Why the writer selected the period of the Persian and Greek domination, he has explained in the first Lecture. He is not unaware of the obscurity of the

* M. Barbier de Meynard.

JEWISH RELIGIOUS LIFE AFTER THE EXILE.

LECTURE I.

Religious Life in Judæa before the Arrival of Nehemiah.

I BRING before you a subject which was not long since in some danger of passing into disrepute. Which of us does not think with pain of the wearisome Scripture history lessons of his childhood? No doubt some improvement has been effected by throwing the light of travel and archæology on the externals of Scripture narratives, but though I congratulate the young scholars of to-day on the greater interestingness of their lessons, I cannot profess to be satisfied. For the unnaturalness of the prevalent conception of Scripture history still remains, and it is not as a collection of picturesque tales that the narratives of the Old Testament will reconquer their position in the educated world. What a modern thinker most desires to learn from the Old Testament is the true history of Jewish religion, and this can only be obtained by applying the methods of modern criticism to the old Hebrew documents. Could this course be adopted, not only in learned academic works, but in popular lectures and handbooks; could the Old Testament be treated in a thoroughly modern spirit, at once sympathetically and critically, I cannot help thinking that this venerable religious record would recover its old fascination. Such is the spirit in which I enter upon this discussion. If I cannot present you with absolute truth, I can at least be sympathetic and critical.

My readers will, I hope, pardon me if I address three requests to them. The first is, that they will meet confidence with confidence, and believe that I have no other object but to tell the reconstructed history of Jewish religion frankly and interestingly, so far as I know it. Next I plead for a renewed study, simultaneously with the reading of this historical sketch, of the letter of the Bible records. And, lastly, I ask that references should be made privately to some good compendium * of the elementary results of mod-

* The two Dictionaries of the Bible, announced by Messrs. T. and F. Clark and Messrs. A. and C. Black, respectively, may be suggested. Some articles in the latter, of which the present writer is one of the editors, are referred to elsewhere in this volume. Vol. I. of the former has just appeared.

ern Biblical criticism. For if I were to be perpetually turning aside to explain such phrases as the Second Isaiah, or to discuss the problems of origin and authorship, the unity of these lectures would be seriously injured, and their object of worthily tracing the history of some phases of a great religion would be proportionally obscured.

I shall not, however, be surprised if some of my readers should smile at my last requirement. I certainly hope that advanced students will expect from me some direct furtherance of critical study, and not merely a repetition of the contents of the handbooks. The subject which I have chosen bristles with critical difficulties, and even a constructive historical sketch may be expected to reveal something of the author's critical basis. It was indeed the difficulty of the subject which partly attracted me; it gives such ample scope for fresh pioneering work. At the same time enough solid results have, as I believe, been obtained to serve as a historical framework. I have also thought that students of this period may be glad to have before them that complex phenomenon which can be explained more fully from the facts of the earlier period. For that epoch a larger amount of material will be at their disposal. They will have not only the Biblical records but also much precious collateral information from Oriental archæology. But in the study of this period I shall generally have to content myself with the post-exilic religious writings, though I am happy in the belief that we understand these to-day much better than we did formerly. Criticism has produced and is still producing results of permanent value, results which it is my hope to weave together and elucidate for historical purposes by the combined use of the two sister faculties—common sense and the imagination.

Let no one indulge in a cheap sarcasm on imaginative criticism: the uses of the imagination are well understood by the greatest of our scientists and historians.* Even in exegesis a happy intuition often pours a flood of light on an obscure passage, and a similar remark is still more applicable to historical reconstruction. These intuitions are not purely accidental. They spring, in exegesis, from sympathy with an author, and a sense of what he can and what he cannot have said; in history, from a sedulously trained imaginative sense of antiquity supported by a large command of facts.

One point more should be frankly stated at the outset. It is, I believe, essential to the investigator of Hebrew antiquity that he should work upon corrected texts, and even to the most modest and unas-

---

* "The imagination. . . . mother of all history as well as of all poetry." Mommsen, *Römische Geschichte*, v. 5.

piring of students that he should have access to translations (more than one, if possible) of such corrected texts. An American professor is now making a brave attempt, with an army of assistants, to meet this want of students, but not much of the result has as yet come under my notice. I have therefore frequently had to give a new translation of my own, based on a corrected text of my own, which I beg you to compare later on with that in Prof. Haupt's Bible.* I now proceed to my subject.

Much uncertainty rests upon the beginning of the post-exilic period. That Cyrus should have wished to restrain members of the Jewish people from returning to the home of their fathers, is against all that we know of his character and principles. The recently discovered cuneiform inscription of Cyrus does not indeed throw any clear light on this matter, but the spirit, which is there ascribed to the great conqueror, is kindly and tolerant. That the disciples of Ezekiel—the first projector, not to say the founder,

---

* The *Polychrome Bible*, edited by Prof. Paul Haupt, of the Johns Hopkins University, Baltimore. The translations from Isaiah in this volume generally agree with the version in the work just referred to; those from the Psalms, with a version, to a large extent based upon a corrected text, which the present writer hopes shortly to publish with justificatory notes. The corrections of the text of Job and Proverbs here adopted, will be found in the *Expositor* for June and July, 1897, and in the *Jewish Quarterly Review* for July and October, 1897, (referred to as *J. Q. R.*).

of the church-nation, a legislator as well as a prophet —should have had no inclination and have made no attempt to carry out their master's legal principles in the Holy Land itself, is scarcely credible. And for those who were both able and willing to take the journey, there was an opportunity presented when Sheshbazzar, or less incorrectly, Sanabassar (as the best Greek authorities give the name), a Babylonian Jew of Davidic descent, was sent to Jerusalem by Cyrus, in accordance with his conciliatory policy, as governor of Judæa. For this high functionary would of course be accompanied by a suite. One of those who went with him was certainly his nephew, Zerubbabel, and it is very possible that the other persons who are mentioned with Zerubbabel in a certain famous list* as "heads" of the Jews in the "province" are really historical. Of those other leaders (eleven in number) the best known is Jeshua or Joshua, who became the first high priest in the post-exilic sense. We must of course suppose that the "heads" went up with their families and dependents, so that they would form altogether a considerable party, though not large enough materially to affect the character of the Judæan community. That as a fact, the party was not in this sense influential, seems to

* Ezr. ii., 2 ; Neh. vii., 7 ; 1 Esdr. v., 8 (where the Greek expresses the term "heads").

me a necessary inference from the prophecies of Haggai and Zechariah.

These prophets had for their aim, to stir the people up to rebuild the ruins of the temple. The work was accomplished, and it is plain from the records that the builders, mostly at any rate, were not returned exiles, but those inhabitants of Judah who had not been carried away by Nebuchadrezzar to Babylon.

Thus in a few words I have stated what I believe to be the truth respecting much debated facts.* The traditional account is, I regret to say, to a large extent untrustworthy. Tradition has partly imagined facts where there were none, partly exaggerated the really existing facts. I must not pause to explain the grounds on which I have made these statements, because my proper subject is not the external but the internal history of the Jews, and the facts which I have stated, to the best of my belief correctly, are to me just now of importance simply as providing the background for certain phases of Jewish religious life. And I at once proceed to ask, What was the religious tone of the unhappy remnant of the old people of Judah?

---

*Compare the article " Israel, History of," in Messrs. A. & C. Black's expected *Encyclopædia Biblica*, and the " Prologue" to Cheyne's *Introduction to the Book of Isaiah*.

The answer is furnished by the prophet Haggai, who, as we have seen, joined Zechariah in a practical appeal to the people of Jerusalem. The response which he met with was by no means encouraging, and the lukewarmness of the citizens seemed to him blameworthy. He lets us see, however, that they reasoned on the subject, and had an excuse for their conduct. They were agriculturists, and had had to contend with a succession of troubles, which seemed to show but too plainly that Jehovah was angry with them, and they declined to take action without a clear sign of his restored favour. " The time is not come," they said," to build the temple of Jehovah"; Jehovah, they thought, would indicate the right time by sending the Messiah. It was only Haggai and Zechariah who, as they themselves believed, understood aright the signs of the times. Even Zerubbabel (who by the year 520 B.C. had succeeded his uncle as governor) and Jeshua, the newly-made high priest, had to be stirred up like the rest, to undertake the work of rebuilding the sacred house. Some sort of house (the term is flexible in Semitic languages) there may for a long time past have been, and this miserable substitute for a temple may have satisfied them. They were doubtless infected by the general despondency, and shrank from the labour and expense of building a true temple, till it was certain that the time had come. Although they had come from Babylon, the headquarters of Jewish piety, they had none of the religious intensity and settled enthusiasm of the disciples of Ezekiel.

I am sorry I cannot give a more romantic story, or gratify the reasonable expectations of students of the Second Isaiah.* The Jews of Judæa at the beginning of our period were poor specimens of religious humanity, and the events of their history are in themselves not very interesting. But the dull periods are necessary as transitions to the bright ones, and surely dull people have their own allotted part, which the historian ought somehow to make interesting. I therefore beg the reader to notice that there was a genuine religious spirit in the poor remnant of Judah, though Haggai thought it very insufficient. We can hardly doubt that, on however slender a scale and with however much ritual irregularity, sacrifices had been persistently offered on the sacred site almost throughout the sad years of the past.† Besides, one of our records incidentally refers to the fact that fasting ‡ had been regularly practised long before

---

* "Second Isaiah" is the name given to the author of the Prophecy of Restoration in Isa. xl.–xlviii.

† The silence of our scanty documents is no evidence to the contrary.

‡ Fasting was one of the most esteemed methods of renewing an impaired connection with the Deity.

520 B.C. The reference occurs in the 7th chapter of Zechariah. The passage well deserves attention; it contains some remarkable statements, and the historical background (to which I shall return later) is really exciting to the imagination.

"In the fourth year of King Darius, on the fourth day of the ninth month Kislev, a divine oracle came to Zechariah. This was the occasion. Bel-sarezer and Raam-melech had sent men to propitiate Jehovah, (and) to ask the priests of Jehovah's house and the prophets this question,—Should I weep in the fifth month abstaining from food, as I have done already so many years? Then it was that this divine oracle came to me, Speak thus to all the people of the land and to the priests."

I break off here in order to bring out three points of some importance. The first is the high position of Zechariah. The days of prophetic authority are numbered, and yet here is a prophet whose words are still law both to the laity and to the priests. The second is the unanimity of the priests of Jehovah and the native Jewish laity as to the high religious worth of fasting. And the third is the fact that the senders of the deputation * (whose real names I can show to be Bel-sarezer and Raam-

---

* They are two of the twelve "heads," who accompanied Sanabassar. See the articles "Sarezer" and "Regem-melech" in the *Encyclopædia Biblica*. Of course, the historical character of Jeshua, and Bilshan (Bel-sarezer), and Raamiah (Regem-melech) only constitutes a *presumption* of the historicity of the other names.

melech) endorse the statement that up to this time (*i. e.*, B.C. 518) the hard lot of the Jews has had no sensible alleviation.

The incident described by Zechariah shows plainly enough that there was no lack of religious feeling at Jerusalem. We may be sure, too, that the little band of religious singers did its best to give expression to this feeling. Very possibly the so-called Lamentations, with the exception of the third, are based on the elegies which were chanted on the commemorative fast-days alluded to by the deputation to Zechariah.

More ancient than this, I cannot venture to make these interesting poems. Striking as the picture of Jeremiah seated on the ruins of Jerusalem and inditing monodies may be, it is too romantic to be true. Delightful as it would be to find at least five works of a virtually pre-exilic religious poet, we must confess that, on internal grounds, the Lamentations in their present form come from a not very early part of the post-exilic period.

Thus, our only authorities for the tone of the earliest post-exilic Judæan religion are the prophecies of Haggai and of the first or true Zechariah. Though devoid of literary charm, they are of much historical importance, because they stand on the dividing line between the exilic and the post-exilic periods. It is a mistaken assertion that the post-exilic age begins with the so-called "edict of Cyrus" in B.C. 537. If there was a post-exilic age at all, it should rather be reckoned from the completion of the second temple in B.C. 516. For the true exile of the Jews was their sense of banishment from their God, and this painful consciousness began to be mitigated as soon as a house had been prepared for Jehovah to dwell in. "It is not time yet to build," said the people of the land, but the prophets believed that the faith and love which the effort of building the temple presupposed would exert a moral attraction upon Jehovah. At any moment after the coping had been laid the King of Glory might be expected to come in. Therefore I say that Haggai and Zechariah inaugurate the post-exilic period.

Nor must we underrate the prophetic gift of these men. They are still, in virtue of their office, the most imposing figures in the community, and they still possess, in some degree, that consciousness of a special relation to God which characterised the great prophets of old. They could have said with Amos, "The Lord Jehovah does nothing without first revealing his secret to his servants the prophets."*

And that very sign of Jehovah's restored favour which the people desiderated, the prophets Haggai

* Am. iii., 7.

and Zechariah believed themselves to have seen—it was the sign of general unrest among the populations of the Persian empire.

Let us first of all see what Haggai, with whom his colleague Zechariah fully agrees, has to declare.

"Yet a little while, saith Jehovah Sabaoth, and I will shake the heavens and the earth and the sea and the dry land ; and I will shake all nations, and the treasures of all nations will come, and I will fill this house with magnificence, saith Jehovah Sabaoth" (Hag. ii., 6, 7).

Two months later another oracle or revelation comes to him,—

"Speak to this effect to Zerubbabel, governor of Judah ; I will shake the heavens and the earth ; I will overthrow royal thrones, and destroy the strength of the kingdoms of the nations. . . . In that day, saith Jehovah Sabaoth, I will take thee, O Zerubbabel my servant, saith Jehovah, and will make thee as a signet ; for I have chosen thee, saith Jehovah Sabaoth" (Hag. ii., 21–23).

The meaning of Haggai is unmistakable. That political insight, by which the prophets interpret the impulses of the spirit, recognises in the disturbances of the peoples the initial stage of the great Judgment Day. The story of these disturbances has been recovered for us by cuneiform research. At the very time when Haggai and Zechariah came forward (it was just after the accession of Darius) revolts were breaking out in different parts of the Persian empire.*

At Babylon, for instance, a man called Nidintu-Bel (*i. e.*, Gift of Bel) had in 521 seized the crown of Nebuchadrezzar, whose name he assumed and whose descendant he professed to be. Now in this pseudo-Nebuchadrezzar, Haggai can hardly have felt a personal interest. But as a sign of the breaking up of the Persian empire he may well have greeted the pretender's appearance with enthusiasm, and when in 519 (soon after Haggai and Zechariah had prophesied so blithely) the revolt of the Babylonians was put down, and when, about 515, a second revolt, led by another pretender,† was extinguished, the leaders of the Jews may be excused if they felt the pangs of disappointment. It had seemed as if a new day were about to dawn, when the glory of Jehovah would again fill his temple, and when Zerubbabel, the Messianic king, would surpass the splendour even of ancient David.

It is a remarkable fact that there is direct evidence

---

* Persia, Susiana, Media, and Babylonia are specially mentioned.

† This second pretender also claimed to be Nebuchadrezzar, son of Nabu-na'id. "It is clear," as Dr. J. P. Peters remarks, "that Nebuchadrezzar was a name to conjure by in Babylonia, so that when a man sought to raise a revolt, he laid claim to this name as a sure means of arousing popular sentiment in his favour." (*Journal of Biblical Literature*, 1897, p. 113.)

Religious Life in Judæa 15

of this in the Bible itself. The prophet Zechariah mentions the arrival at Jerusalem of four Jews (probably the leaders of a party) with gifts of silver and gold from the wealthy Babylonian settlements. The treasure was converted, in accordance with a divine direction, into a crown for Zerubbabel.* This Davidic prince, be it remembered, had already received the Messianic name Branch or Sprout † which had been coined perhaps by Jeremiah, and all that remained was to anoint him and announce his accession to the people. Whether the public announcement was ever made in a form which could be called treasonable, we know not. But it is not improbable that a later editor, who did not comprehend the passage and wished to suggest a possible historical reference, has put the name of Joshua instead of Zerubbabel into the text.

There is yet another historical fact which deserves to be mentioned. It is recorded in Ezr. v.—and I see no reason here for scepticism—that Tatnai or Sisines, the satrap of Syria, endeavoured to stop the building of the temple; I am inclined to bring this fact into connection with the sudden disappearance of Zerubbabel. This prince was no doubt a Persian

---

* Zech. vi., 9-12, where read in ver. 11, "make crowns, and set them on the heads of Zerubbabel." The text has suffered corruption. See article "Zerubbabel" in Messrs. A. & C. Black's *Encyclopædia Biblica*, where another possible view is indicated.

† Zech. iii., 8 ; *cf.* vi., 12.

governor, but he was also by birth and religion a Jew, and we should have expected to find him, and not Bel-sarezer and Raam-melech, sending that deputation to the temple which is referred to by Zechariah. The fact that two inferior functionaries, and not Zerubbabel, are mentioned, suggests the idea that the latter may have been suspected of treason, and have been recalled by Darius, and the additional fact that the satrap Tatnai sought to stop the building of the temple is equally suggestive of a belief in the disloyalty of the Jews. It is a further confirmation of this theory that we find Sanballat warning Nehemiah that he was in danger of being informed against, on account of prophetic announcements that there was a king in Judah (Neh. vi., 7).

I cannot help feeling a reverent pity for the disillusionment of Zechariah, and a respect for his truthfulness in not omitting to record his mistake. True, it is not quite impossible that he minimised his error. He may have considered that he had only been mistaken as to the time of the fulfilment of the prophecy, and have clung to his belief in Zerubbabel's Messianic character. But the sense of even a partial mistake must have been painful, and we are not surprised at the want of enthusiasm which marks his reply to the deputation. The reported objects of the embassy are equally suggestive of mental depression. One of them was "to propitiate Jehovah," which implies that Jehovah was not considered altogether friendly, and another, to ask a question about fasting, designed apparently to extract from the prophets some word of good cheer for the future. The laity, it seems, would gladly have given up commemorative fast-days if only they could have been sure that "the Lord whom they sought" would speedily "come to his temple." The question was asked before the fast of the fifth month, but Zechariah delayed his oracular response till the fast of the seventh month was over. It is evident that he felt the difficulty of the religious situation. The inward calm required in a recipient of the prophetic afflatus but slowly returned to him. His reply, when it came, was twofold. First, he assured the people, in the spirit of Isaiah, that Jehovah cared not whether they fasted, or not. Next, he told them that Jehovah was keenly interested in his people, and would certainly return, to which he added an exhortation to obey the moral precepts of the old prophets, such as Isaiah and Jeremiah. He did not however make it sufficiently clear that, according to the old prophets, no salvation could come to an unreformed people, and Haggai is not reported to have given any such moral exhortation at all.

Great prophets they certainly are not; their literary style is miserable, and their spirit shows a sad falling off as compared with that of the older prophets. Zechariah is the greater of the two, but even he is deficient in moral energy, and shows traces of a doctrine which in the hands of a weak moralist may be most injurious,—I mean, dualism. He thinks that the colossal calamity of Israel is due to the agency of a heavenly being called the Satan, whose function it is to remind God of human sins which he might otherwise be glad to forget. This notion might have been harmless if it had been coupled with the belief (which we find in the great Elihu-poem inserted in the Book of Job) that there was also another angelic agent whose business it was to save sinners by leading them to repentance (Job xxxiii., 23, 24). But not being so coupled, it led to a weakened view of moral responsibility and of the need of moral reformation. We also find Zechariah making a singular misuse of the poetic faculty of personification. He regards the wickedness of his countrymen as too great to be the product of mere human nature. There must, he thinks, be an evil principle called Wickedness, which causes all this superabundance of iniquity. And in a vision (Zech. v., 5–11) he actually sees this principle incarnate in the form of a woman, who is seated in a vessel of a ton weight, and is then suddenly thrown down, while the lid is shut to. Then she is borne by two women with storks' wings to the land of Shinar (*i. e.*, Babylonia) that she may dwell there, and so bring the ruin upon Babylonia which she now threatens to bring upon the land of the Jews.

Still from this time forward we notice a steady expectation of the coming of Jehovah to judgment, and the deficiencies of Zechariah as an ethical preacher are made good by a subsequent prophet, who has not cared for posthumous fame, and has written anonymously. Subsequent generations, through an odd mistake, gave him the name of Malachi.

"Behold, the day comes," he exclaims, "burning as an oven ; all the arrogant and all wicked-doers will become like stubble ; the day that comes will burn them root and branch. But upon you, the fearers of my name, the sun of righteousness will dawn with healing in his wings ; ye will go forth and grow fat like calves of the stall. Ye will tread down the wicked ; they will become ashes under the soles of your feet, in the day when I carry out my promise, saith Jehovah Sabaoth."

Then, apparently as the condition of the preceding promise, he adds, " Remember ye the law of my servant Moses, to whom I gave in charge in Horeb statutes and judgments for all Israel " (Mal. iv., 3).

Evidently the tide had begun to turn ; the rebuilding of the temple marks a historical epoch. However faulty the popular religion might be,—and Malachi does not stint himself in his denunciation of it—there was more spiritual life in the community than in Haggai's time. There were not a few at any rate who were strict observers of the Deuteronomic Law, and who by their conscientiousness atoned for the laxity of the multitude. All that these men needed to make their witness efficacious was qualified leaders, in whom theoretical insight and practical ability were united. Such capable men were indeed to be found, but in the lands of the Dispersion, not in Judæa. How is this to be accounted for? Why did they remain in their distant homes? Why did not more Israelites return?

Some, I make no doubt, did return. It is clear from Zechariah that Babylonian Jews sometimes came on visits to the holy city, and it is hardly credible that none of these were induced to lay down their pilgrim-staves, and remain in Jerusalem. Such immigrants would naturally attach themselves to the "fearers of Jehovah" whom they already found there,—that is, to those strict observers of Deuteronomy who had formed themselves, as Malachi tells us (iii., 16), into an association. But the general aspect of the population was not appreciably affected by these few immigrants. The Judæans, as a late prophetic writer says, were like a poor-looking cluster of grapes, which the vintager only spares for the sake of the few good grapes which hang upon it (Isa. lxv). So, again I ask, Why did not more Israelites return?

Three plausible answers may be given. (1) Since the fall of the ancient state there had been a great gulf between the Babylonian and the Judæan Israelites. Both Jeremiah and Ezekiel use the most disparaging language of the Jews who did not share the fate of Jehoiachin, and the Second Isaiah even ignores the Jews in Judæa altogether. (2) Strong Jewish colonies in other parts of the empire were important both as increasing the influence of the race, and as providing the silver and gold for religious uses in which the scanty Judæan population was deficient. Nor must the religious value of their witness for ethical monotheism be forgotten. (3) The predictions of the Second Isaiah assumed that the powers of heaven and earth were united in favour of Israel's restoration, whereas at present both the heavenly and the earthly voices were, as it seemed, obstinately silent.

In course of time, God put it into the heart of one of the Jewish priests in Babylonia to head a migration to Judæa. But there were men of a different school who, before this, had as it seems made an effort to stimulate the Babylonian Jews. We have, not improbably, a record of this attempt in chaps. xlix–lv., of the Book of Isaiah, which appear to be an appendix to the original Prophecy of Restoration, written in Babylonia by an admirer of the Second Isaiah, and brought to Jerusalem. Almost throughout this section the point of view is shifted from Babylon and the exiles to Zion and its struggling community. Indeed, but for the beauty of the style, and the delicacy of the art, by which these chapters contrast with those which were undeniably appended at Jerusalem (chaps. lx–lxii.) and but for the want of concreteness and I may even say the inappropriateness in the descriptions of the Zion community, we might bring ourselves to suppose that they were written in Judæa. The phenomena may be best reconciled by the theory that the chapters were written in Babylonia, partly to induce Babylonian Jews to go to Judæa, partly to encourage hard-pressed workers in Jerusalem.

Allow me to quote a very familiar passage, which however is too generally misunderstood through not being furnished with the right historical background.*

* See Isaiah in the *Polychrome Bible*, and *cf. Introduction to Isaiah* by the present writer; see also article " Isaiah " in the *Encyclopædia Biblica*.

"Ho! all ye that are athirst, go to the waters,
And ye that have no strength, eat!
Go, buy grain without money,
Wine and milk without price.
Why do ye pay money for that which is no bread,
And take trouble for that which satisfies not?" (Isa. lv., 1, 2).

Here the "waters," the "grain," the "wine," and the "milk," are all those blessings, both moral and material, the reception of which can effect the regeneration of a people. It is presupposed that an organised community exists in the land of Israel, and it is the pious preacher's wish to stir up devout men in Babylonia to claim their share in the life and work of this community. Unless, either in a figure or, best of all, in reality, they go to Jerusalem, they will continue, he thinks, to be like the "dry bones" of another prophet's vision. They may have money to spend, but there is no bread for them to buy. They may "rise up early and late take rest,"* but they will have no satisfaction from their gains. They are, by their own choice, "strangers to the commonwealth of Israel." Better far were it to join the ranks of Jehovah's confessors,—for such, the writer mistakenly assumes, the Jews of Judæa have become; better far were it to suffer the insulting of men, which will last but for a moment, and

* Ps. cxxvii., 3. (Prayerbook version.)

to wait at Zion for that awakening of the arm of Jehovah which will renew the wonders of the days of old. Sore need has desolate Zion of her children; when will the exiles in a body depart in a holy procession from Babylon—not in flight, as the Second Isaiah had formerly said, but in grave, majestic solemnity, with Jehovah for their protector both in the van and in the rear?*

Of the two very different gifts for which Jerusalem had lately been indebted to Babylon—the treasure made into a crown for Zerubbabel and the first appendix to the Prophecy of Restoration, the former was much more easy to make use of than the latter. The golden crown was no doubt melted down, and converted into some needed ornament for the temple. But the new prophetic rhapsody was too idealistic to be greatly appreciated at Jerusalem. Ezekiel was at that time much more likely to influence "church-workers." His conception of "holiness" and his horror of profane contact with holy things are to be found both in Zechariah and in Malachi (Zech. iii., 7, Mal. ii., 11). It is also from Ezekiel that the distinction between priests and Levites traceable in the ancient list of the "children of the province" (Ezr. ii., Neh. vii.) is derived, and it is Ezekiel who has set the tone and suggested some of

* Isa. li., 7–10; liv., 1; lii., 12.

Religious Life in Judæa 25

the chief details of perhaps the earliest of the prophecies in the third part of Isaiah (Isa. lvi. 9–lvii. 13a).

The prophecy to which I have referred is one which loses greatly through being read in a poor translation of an uncorrected text. Its true meaning and that of the related prophecies in Isa. lxv., lxvi., 1–22 deserves to be better known. The persons so angrily attacked by the prophetic writers are the half-Jews of central Palestine commonly called Samaritans, and those Jews in Judæa and Jerusalem who had more or less religious sympathy with them. How it is possible that the bitter feelings expressed in these passages can ever have been imputed to the suave and affectionate Second Isaiah, it is difficult to conceive. Even one of the earlier post-exilic prophets, such as Haggai or Zechariah, could not have written such angry invectives. For the truth is, that there is no evidence that in the earlier period there was any strong religious feud between the Jews and the Samaritans. The Samaritans were doubtless farther off from legal orthodoxy than the Jews, but the standard of orthodoxy even among the Jews cannot have been very high, especially in the country districts, where, in the absence of a strong central authority, gross superstitions still lingered. Nor is there any reason to think that the Samaritans ever gave up their interest in the great sanctuary of Judah until they were forced. It is said that not long after the burning of the temple a party of eighty pilgrims came from Shechem, Shiloh, and Samaria to Mizpah bringing offerings for the old sanctuary there,* and if the temple of Jerusalem had not been in ruins, they would no doubt have preferred it to the sanctuary of Mizpah.† We need not therefore doubt that when in 520 the Jews determined to rebuild their temple, the Samaritans felt a sympathetic interest in the undertaking. They might not care to relieve the Jews of the duty of rebuilding their sanctuary (the story of their interfering with their kinsmen under pretence of a wish to co-operate, is a pure imagination,) but when by Zechariah's contagious enthusiasm the work had been done, they would naturally be eager to maintain their connection with such a holy place. By the aid of the priestly aristocracy they succeeded in doing this till Nehemiah, armed with a Persian firman, interposed.

The course of action which this great official adopted provoked the Samaritans to the utmost, and radically changed their relations to the Jews. We may be inclined to blame Nehemiah until we remem-

* Jer. xli., 5. The sad story of the pilgrims is hardly less horrible than that of the well at Cawnpore in India.

† Many writers think that the "house of Jehovah" referred to in Jeremiah really means the ruin-laden site of the temple of Jerusalem.

ber that the religious isolation of the Jews on a strictly legal basis was an object of vital importance to the higher religion, and that an attempt had already been made by orthodox Jews to convert the Samaritans. On this attempt a few words of explanation seem necessary. It is recorded, as I believe, in the following passage from the work of a prophetic writer of the time preceding Nehemiah, who belonged to the orthodox school * :

"I offered admission to those who asked not after me; I offered my oracles to those who sought me not; I said, Here am I, here am I, to a class of men which called not upon my name. I have spread out my hands all the day to an unruly and disobedient people, who follow the way which is not good, after their own devices" (Isa. lxv., 1, 2).

This I take to mean that some of the orthodox leaders of the Jews wished to make the continued admission of the Samaritans to religious privileges (and to all that this involved) conditional on their renunciation of their distinguishing peculiarities and their adoption of the Jewish law and traditions. They attempted, in a word, to make converts of the Samaritans, but the attempt was a failure. Probably enough, there were faults on both sides. The Jews were deficient in suavity, like Augustine of Canterbury when he tried in vain to unite the English and

* It was Prof. Duhm of Basel who first pointed this out.

the Welsh in one Christian Church; the Samaritans, on their side, had as yet no religious receptivity. And now a most strange phenomenon meets us, though not more so than many which we shall encounter in the later literature, not more so, for instance, than the fact that "Malachi," violently opposed as he is to an intermingling of races in the Jewish territory, grasps the fundamental reforming principle of the divine fatherhood, and asserts the universality of a true worship of Jehovah.* The phenomenon to which I refer is this,—that the same writer (probably) who has just spoken so harshly of the Samaritans because they have refused to adopt the Jewish law, now censures them for wishing to build a central sanctuary of their own, and bases this censure on a principle which, regarded logically, is just as adverse to the claims of the temple at Jerusalem. He says:

Thus saith Jehovah; Heaven is my throne and earth my footstool. What house would ye build for me, and what place as my habitation? For all this has my hand made, and mine is all this, saith Jehovah. (Isa. lxvi., 1,2.)

The explanation is that post-exilic Jewish religion is to a large extent a fusion of inconsistent elements, of prophetic and priestly origin, respectively. Upon one side of his nature this writer, like many another,

* Mal. ii., 10, 11; i., 11.

sympathises with prophets like Jeremiah; upon another, with the priests. Experience proved that it was hopeless to refound the Judæan community on pure prophetic spiritualism; traditional forms had to be retained, and so far as possible rendered harmless or symbolic of spiritual truth. And so this writer, though he holds that not even the temple at Jerusalem is worthy of the Divine Creator, yet expostulates with those who plan the erection of another temple elsewhere. It is only in the temple so lately rebuilt that the right worshippers are to be found, viz., the humble and obedient Jewish believers. Let the Samaritans renounce their self-chosen and often abominable customs, and submit to the Law, and then it will be permitted to them to worship God in a temple made with hands.

Into the details of the customs ascribed to the opponents of orthodoxy (viz., the Samaritans and the least advanced of the old Jewish remnant) it is not necessary to enter. (See Isa. lxv., 3-5, 11; lxvi., 3, 4.) But it is interesting to see how orthodox Jews at this period expressed their aversion to those opponents in sacred song. I quote from a fragment of an old post-exilic psalm which seems to have received a later addition; it is the kernel of our present 16th psalm.*

* I translate from a corrected text.

Keep watch over me, O God, for in thee I take refuge !
I profess to Jehovah, Thou art my Lord ;
To draw near to thee is my happiness,
And in thy holy seasons is all my delight.

Those who choose another (than Jehovah) give themselves much pain ;
Their libations of blood I will not pour out ;
Their (deity's) names I will not take on my lips,
Jehovah (alone) is my cup's portion and my lot.
(Ps. xvi., 1–5.)

To understand the allusions we must refer to different passages in the third part of Isaiah written in the age of Nehemiah, most probably shortly before his arrival. The speaker is the personified association of pious Israelites, which, however small, feels itself the bearer of Jehovah's banner, and contrasts its own inward happiness and assured glorification with the present spiritual loss and future punishment of those who indulge in the abominable rites of the Samaritans.

It may perhaps be objected to the foregoing sketch of the early dealings of the Jews and the Samaritans that it is a reconstruction of history. It is so, and it ought to be so. That the right moment for such an attempt has arrived, no one who knows the course of recent criticism can deny, and historical students will, I believe, recognise that the results here given have considerable probability. It has at any rate been shown that the feud between the Jews and the Samaritans was probably of later and more gradual origin than has been supposed, and that the plan of building a Samaritan temple arose long before the time of Alexander the Great, when, according to Josephus, the Gerizim-sanctuary was erected. And hence the question arises, May not Josephus have been mistaken as to the date of this event?*

It is admitted that he places the expulsion of Sanballat's son-in-law Manasseh (to which I shall refer again) a hundred years too late; why, then, should we assume that he is more correct in a closely related statement? It is true, he repeats the statement as to the date of the temple elsewhere; but cannot a writer be persistently inaccurate? The chronology of the Persian period was, in Josephus's time, so obscure that he may well be pardoned for such an error.

A word may be added in conclusion with regard to Manasseh. The complete story of this Jewish priest will be given later. He incurred the special displeasure of Nehemiah because under aggravating circumstances he had contracted a mixed marriage. But we must not take too low a view of Manasseh's

---

* Jos. Ant., xi., 8, 2-4. The inaccuracy is of course diminished if, as some think, it was the second and not the first Artaxerxes under whose patronage Nehemiah and Ezra came to Jerusalem.

character. Belonging as he did to the old Jerusalem priesthood, he had his own views of what became a priest, and his own way of interpreting the Law, and though Malachi would have said that he had "caused many to stumble" by his interpretation (Mal. ii., 8), yet we shall see presently that the rigorous views of Ezra and Nehemiah were not the only ones represented among faithful Jews. Certain it is that he was very different religiously from his friends the Samaritans, and that Nehemiah really benefited the rival community by forcing Manasseh to take refuge among them. Manasseh, as it would seem, became the religious reformer of the Samaritans. Quite possibly he took with him, on his expulsion, not merely the Book of Deuteronomy, but the whole Pentateuch in the form in which it then existed. We may assume that he also obtained the erection of the temple of Gerizim, and so achieved the centralisation of the Samaritan worship.

Thus the fugitive Jewish priest Manasseh became the greatest benefactor of the Samaritan community. To him alone it is indebted for its long survival. The temple built (as I believe) through him was destroyed by the Hasmonæan sovereign of Judæa, John Hyrcanus, in B.C. 130. It was succeeded by a temple at Shechem which no doubt perished when the town of Shechem was laid in ruins by Vespasian. But the Samaritans continued to cling to the neighbourhood of their sacred mountain, and some of us may even have seen the old paschal rites celebrated on a sacred spot on Gerizim, which was perhaps within the precincts of Manasseh's temple. The Samaritans may, from a modern theological point of view, be simply a Jewish sect, but, putting ourselves in their intellectual position, we cannot be surprised if they consider their local continuance as the strongest of arguments in favour of their religious orthodoxy. They may be an insignificant minority of the worshippers of the God of Jacob, but a sign from the supernatural world would in a moment change the relative position of Jews and Samaritans, as indeed unreformed Judaism itself teaches that a supernatural interposition will one day invert the relations of Jews and Gentiles. Jehovah Nissi (Jehovah is my Banner) might therefore be taken as a motto not less by the depressed community at Nâblus than by that almost œcumenical body—the Jewish Church.

For after all, Jews and Samaritans alike have a grasp of the truth: we only part from them, or from any of our fellow-Christians, in so far as they mix up the truth with arrogant and unspiritual assumptions. They base their right to existence on their faith, and faith is indeed the only rock which will uphold either communities or individuals in the sea of change. I venture to claim a right to say this even in a historical discussion, because to inquire about religions without experimental knowledge of the essence of religion seems to me an unprofitable pastime. Faith is the essence of religion on its heavenward side, and the Chronicler rightly discerned the connecting link between the religion of the pre-exilic prophets and that of the post-exilic Church when he imagined King Jehoshaphat thus addressing the assembled congregation in the wilderness of Tekoa:

"Hear me, O Judah, and ye inhabitants of Jerusalem. Believe Jehovah your God, so shall ye be established; believe his prophets, so shall ye prosper." (2 Chr. xx., 20.)

For the pre-exilic prophet Isaiah had long before intuitively made the discovery which was a religious commonplace to the Chronicler, when he said to Ahaz and his courtiers, "If ye will not believe, then ye shall not be established."* (Isa. vii., 9.) And it is on this firm ground, and not on any subtle theory of the nature of Inspiration or the interpretation of formularies, that I base my own personal right to go as deep as I can in Biblical research, and my advocacy of a braver and a bolder policy than has yet been common in the instruction of students. Such a policy can do no one's religion any real harm, and, in my

* Or, "If ye will not hold fast (*i. e.*, to the living God), then ye shall not be held fast."

Religious Life in Judæa

opinion, accords best with the spirit of One whom I am not worthy to name, but who is the Master and Leader of all who are seeking to purify the moral and religious conceptions of the Church or the community.

It is the attitude of the Master towards the Jewish Law which justifies Christian critics (for whom I now write) in their free but reverent attitude towards the historical documents of the Church, among which those of the Old and the New Testament stand supreme. How much the religion of mankind owes to the reverent but incomparably bold attitude of the Master towards the Jewish Law, can already be seen in part, and at a later stage of the world's history will be discerned more fully. And the reader will rightly suppose that my treatment of the Samaritans in this historical sketch is partly suggested by the mild reasonableness of the Master's estimate of that people. The disparaging sentiment of the ancient Jews respecting them is well known. But the Master on two occasions * contrasted the moral and religious practice of the Jews and of the Samaritans to the advantage of the latter. If this was just and right in the Roman period of Jewish history, it cannot be plausible to assume that the Samaritans of Nehemiah's age were entirely destitute of the essential qualities of human goodness.

* Luke x., 33; xvii., 16.

LECTURE II.

Nehemiah, Ezra, and Manasseh; or, The Reconstitution of the Jewish and the Samaritan Communities.

WE have, I hope, already gained some valuable results. That a fugitive Jewish priest became the reformer of the Samaritan religion, is not the least interesting of them, and accordingly I shall endeavour to place this fact in its right setting. First of all, however, permit me to direct your attention to some patriotic enterprises of Babylonian and Judæan Israelites which preceded the expulsion of Manasseh. It is certain that the Jews who remained in Babylonia had by no means forgotten Jerusalem. Though they did not migrate to Judæa, they must have had such a migration in view, for the *élite* of their body devoted themselves to the difficult task of bringing the traditional Jewish laws up to date. To this truly patriotic enterprise I shall have to refer later on. A not less important work, undertaken in Babylonia, was that of supplementing and adapting the fragments of early prophecies to the needs of the present. As I have already mentioned, the author of the first appendix to the Second Isaiah's prophecy (chaps. xlix.–lv.) endeavoured to stimulate Babylonian Jews to a personal co-operation with the Judæan reformers. This eloquent writer was evidently in close touch with those faithful workers. He knew their difficulties, and had noted with regret their liability to fits of discouragement. Like them, he longed to see a general return of the Jewish exiles, but he felt that, to bring this about, Jehovah himself must beckon with his mighty hand to the nations.* To this great event he pointed his readers with confidence.

But a far more practical idea suggested itself to a Judæan Israelite named Hanani. Possibly he was an official of some kind; at any rate, he afterwards filled an office of much consideration at Jerusalem (Neh. vii., 2). It was his good fortune to be related to Nehemiah, one of the butlers of King Artaxerxes,† and he induced a party of Judæans to accompany him on a visit to his influential kinsman. On his arrival at Susa (the winter residence of the Persian kings), he told Nehemiah, in reply to a question, how miserable a state Jerusalem was in, and he connected this misery with an outrage which might

* Isa. xlix., 22.
† Artaxerxes Longimanus (466–448 B.C.), as most critics suppose.

almost appear to be a recent one, if there were anything in the rest of the document to justify the supposition. These are the words of the question and answer, as Nehemiah in his brief way reports them:

" I asked them respecting the Jews that had escaped, who remained over from the captivity, and respecting Jerusalem. And they said to me, those who remain over from the captivity there in the province are greatly afflicted and insulted ; the wall of Jerusalem is broken down, and its gates are burned." (Neh. i., 2, 3.)

Nehemiah was conscious that a crisis had arrived, and that it devolved upon him to make a supreme effort for the good of Jerusalem. He was no mere theorist, and could not think it sufficient to write addresses full of a soaring but impracticable idealism. What he did, or at least wishes us to know that he did, is recorded in his autobiography. This document is one of our best authorities; its preservation is a piece of singular good fortune. Still there are some questions of the historical student which it fails to answer. It does not, for instance, explain how Artaxerxes came to be more friendly to the Jews than either Cyrus or Darius. Evidently there was some political motive for this king's generosity, and it is the business of the historian to divine it. I venture therefore to make a conjecture. In 448 B.C. there was a very serious revolt of the Syrian satrap Megabyzos. It is more than probable that the Jews avoided being drawn into this, and we may presume that Artaxerxes wished to reward them for their loyalty. I believe that Nehemiah understood this state of things, and even suspected that he owed his position at court, which in former times had been filled by high-born Persian nobles, to the philo-Judaism of Artaxerxes. Not improbably too some of the chief men of Jerusalem were as well informed as Nehemiah, so that the arrival of Hanani and his companions was not quite so accidental as Josephus in his romantic narrative represents it * (Jos. Ant. xi., 5, 6).

One fact at any rate is certain,—that Nehemiah obtained leave of absence to go to Jerusalem in the capacity of governor, with the special object of repairing the walls. With firman and military escort he hurried to the holy city. Arrived there, he at once showed his characteristic self-reliance. He might have called the notables together, and have asked their opinion as to the expediency of rebuilding the walls. But there were great divisions among the citizens, some of whom, members of the priestly class as well as laymen, were closely connected with

---

* The Judæans may have long desired to repair the walls of their capital, but have not felt sure enough of their favour at court to ask leave to do so.

the Samaritan leaders. Nehemiah doubtless knew this, and was unwilling to incur the risk of having his own opinion rejected. So the third night after his arrival he and a few trusty followers partly rode, partly walked, round the walls of the city.* At such a time as this (though, most probably, a hundred years or more later), a psalmist wrote these words, which well express the feelings of Nehemiah:

"For thy servants take pleasure in her stones,
  And are distressed to see her in the dust."
                                    (Ps. cii., 14.)

Stirred in his inmost depths, the governor now called the notables together. He told them how plainly the hand (*i. e.*, the providence) of God had been over him. Opposition was impossible. Eliashib, the friend of a leading Samaritan, was foremost among Nehemiah's supporters. It was like the rebuilding of the wall of Athens after the Persian invasion. In fifty-two days the wall was completely repaired.†

The truth of the story cannot be doubted. We have indeed a partial parallel for it in the story of a not less egotistic and not less meritorious officer in the Persian service, the Egyptian priest Uza-hor. Under two of the last native kings of Egypt this

* Neh. ii., 11-15.
† Neh. ii., 17, 18 ; iii., 1 ; vi., 15.

man had been admiral of the fleet, but upon the conquest of Egypt by Cambyses he received the post of a chief physician. He was more than this, however. His father had been chief priest of the august mother of the sun-god, the goddess Nît, whose chief temple was at Saïs. Uza-hor took advantage of his position at the Persian court to instil into the king a high notion of the dignity of his goddess, and of the duty of purifying her temple, and restoring her cultus in its beauty. Cambyses recognised the duty, and gave orders to restore the worship of Nît. He himself even testified his reverence for the great goddess, like all pious kings of Egypt before him. "He did this," says Uza-hor, "because I had made known to him the high importance of the holy goddess." So skilfully did Uza-hor reconcile his duty as a courtier with his obligations to his religion. And that he was no mere ritualist, is shown by his attention to those works of mercy which were so much regarded in ancient Egypt. "I protected the people," he says, "in the very sore calamity which had happened throughout the land. I sheltered the weak from the strong. I gave to the destitute a good burial, I nourished all their children, and built up again all their houses." Then came the accession of Darius, who extended the same favour to Uza-hor, and sent him to Egypt to reappoint the holy scribes of the temples in full numbers, and to restore everything that had fallen into decay. "I did as I was commanded," says Uza-hor. "I took children, I confided them to expert masters in all branches of knowledge. Those who distinguished themselves I provided with all that they required as scribes. O ye divinities of Saïs! remember all the good that Uza-hor the chief physician has done! O Osiris, do unto him all that is good, even as he has done it who is the guardian of thy shrine for evermore."*

This Egyptian document is in several respects of considerable importance. First, it exemplifies the respectful attitude of the Persian kings towards the religions of conquered races. The Achæmenian dynasty was not religiously intolerant except towards the end of its time, nor did it care to proselytise in countries like Egypt, Babylonia, and Palestine, which had religions of ancient and reputable lineage. Indeed, the monuments show that marked favour was extended by Cyrus to the Babylonians, and by Cambyses and Darius to the Egyptians. For this there were special reasons of high state policy, and I have suggested that the favour of Artaxerxes to the Jews should be similarly accounted for. But of course the influence of friendly officials was an indispensable help. It was a blessing for the Egyptians that Uza-

* Brugsch, *Gesch. Äg.*, pp. 784 *ff.*

hor filled the post of chief physician, and no less for the Jews that Nehemiah filled that of royal butler. We may be sure that the latter took care to oil the political wheels by representing the Jews as loyal subjects and as akin to the Persians by the purity and sublimity of their religion.

Next, the egotistic language of the Egyptian courtier of Darius is remarkable, because it reminds us of the egotism of the Jewish courtier of Artaxerxes. But there is this difference between the two. Nehemiah's egotism is a quality which is new among Israelites, while Uza-hor does but carry on the tradition of Egyptian courtiers of many centuries. In fact, Egypt was far in advance of Israel in moral development. The individualism which marks the Hebrew Book of Proverbs, which is post-exilic, characterised the Precepts of the Egyptian prince Ptah-hotep long before; no wonder, then, that the egotism of Nehemiah should have much earlier parallels in the inscriptions on Egyptian statues. Nor is it a digression to remind you that the Egyptians, since a remote antiquity, had looked forward to a judgment after death with rewards and punishments for the individual. The inscriptions on the statues (which are in tomb-chapels) are addressed chiefly to the gods. We can hardly say the like of Nehemiah's account of his good deeds. But he is evidently thinking of a future reward, when he pauses in the midst of his story to ejaculate the prayer, "Remember me, O my God, for good." * Is this merely a "prayer for posthumous fame?" Dean Stanley thought so.† But surely the words are to be explained by that touching utterance of a psalmist:

> "Remember me, Jehovah, when thou showest favour to thy people,
> Take notice of me when thou workest deliverance,
> That I may feast mine eyes on the felicity of thy chosen,
> May rejoice in the joy of thy nation,
> May share the triumph of thine inheritance."
>
> (Ps. cvi., 4, 5.)

Nehemiah hopes in fact to have brought the Messianic period a good deal nearer by the trouble he has taken, and has dreams of being as prominent then as he has been at this critical time at Jerusalem.

Certainly the butler of Artaxerxes was the one great man in Judæa. Though not quite devoid of idealism, he showed a promptitude both in counsel and in action which reminds us of Napoleon. That he was impatient and masterful, is but a way of saying that he was extremely able and knew his own ability. The times demanded such a man, and any

---

* Neh. v., 19; xiii., 14, 22, 31.
† *Lectures on the Jewish Church*, iii., 120.

other living Jew would probably have failed. If I add that he hated the opponents of orthodox religion with an intensity that shocks us, and that he suspected them of meanness as well as of religious error,—that will not surprise any thoughtful student. It was difficult—if not impossible—in those early times to love God fervently without hating a large section of God's creatures. What Nehemiah's feelings were towards the races outside Palestine, we can only conjecture, but we know that he detested three persons, Sanballat the Horonite, Tobiah the Ammonite, and Geshem or Gashmu the Arabian.

This detestation was of course not peculiar to Nehemiah. Shortly before his arrival prophets had written in the most bitter terms respecting the Samaritans.* The relations between the two kindred communities were becoming more and more strained. Sanballat and Tobiah, worshippers of the same God as orthodox Jews, had come to feel that the differences which parted them were greater than the resemblances which united them. And when Nehemiah arrived, " it grieved them exceedingly that there was come a man " to give—as it appeared—a final preponderance to the orthodox party at Jerusalem, or as Nehemiah himself expresses it, "to seek the welfare of the Israelites." † And they had good reason.

* Isa. lvii., 3–13 ; lxv. ; lxvi. † Neh. ii., 10.

The prophets who had written against the Samaritans had done so anonymously. It was Nehemiah who made the first official declaration of war. "We are the servants of the God of heaven; but ye have no portion, nor right, nor memorial in Jerusalem."* Let me repeat. It was not originally the Samaritans who wished to be separate from the Jews. Gladly would they have resorted to the sanctuary at Jerusalem, and after death have enjoyed that shadowy immortality which consisted in having a monument in the holy city.† But Nehemiah and the exclusive party knew their own mind, and emphasised their hostility to their neighbours by repairing the wall of Jerusalem, not so much as a protection against ordinary foes as to keep out the Samaritans.

The Samaritans on their side affected to be astonished at Nehemiah for venturing to commit an act of overt rebellion against Persia.‡ Some of the Jewish prophets had in all probability given them some excuse for this bold misrepresentation. The statement comes to us from Sanballat, but there is no sufficient reason to suppose that it was a pure fiction of the Samaritan leader. We know that Haggai and Zechariah had put forward Zerubbabel as the Mes-

---

* Neh. ii., 20.

† *Cf.* Isa. lvi., 9, "a memorial and a name better than sons and daughters." ‡ Neh. ii., 19.

sianic king, and it is probable enough that other prophets in Nehemiah's time declared this great man (the one great man in Judæa, as I have said) to be the Messiah. It is true, Nehemiah was not a descendant of David. But it is not certain that Jeremiah and Ezekiel, when they speak of David or of a Sprout of David as the future ideal king, mean to insist on a literal descent from the son of Jesse. If a hero who came with the spirit and power of David had been put before them, it is probable that they would have recognised in him a true son of David, just as Jesus recognised in the appearance of John the Baptist the fulfilment of the well-known prophecy of Malachi.* The Samaritans, then, had really a specious pretext for setting the story about Nehemiah afloat. Jewish prophets had for a moment connected the governor's name with the traditional Messianic hope. But Nehemiah himself † was too wise and too honest to permit such preaching, and so to fan the delusive hope of Judæan independence. And I suspect that Sanballat understood this. It is hardly conceivable that the governor's primary object in building the walls can have remained a secret to Sanballat.

What that object was we have seen already. Ne-

---

* Matt. xi., 14; Mark ix., 13; *cf.* Luke i., 17.
† Neh. vi., 7.

hemiah wished to defend Jerusalem from the attack which the Samaritans would probably make on the city (on the pretext of Nehemiah's rebellion against his liege lord), when the right of worshipping in the temple and of intermarrying with the Jews had been withdrawn from them. One point however must be mentioned to the credit of Sanballat. Before the doors of the city were set into the gates, he made a final attempt to effect a compromise with Nehemiah.* The governor, it is true, declares in his memoirs that the Samaritans had a plot against him. But the fact that Sanballat, undeterred by Nehemiah's first refusal, made four more attempts to arrange a conference speaks in his favour. The governor's rudeness was enough to provoke any one, and goes some way to excuse the final insult of Sanballat. That bold man only threw a doubt publicly on Nehemiah's loyalty in revenge for repeated and most unseemly rebuffs; his earlier efforts for a compromise were made in good faith. That Nehemiah did not believe this, is no decisive argument on his side. His acuteness was preternatural. He scented treachery everywhere, and would not trust his nearest neighbours. A prophet urges him to take refuge in the sanctuary. At once he infers that the prophet is in the pay of Sanballat (Neh. vi., 10-14). The nobles of Jerusalem

* Neh. vi., 1-9.

keep up a correspondence with their old friend and the kinsman of some of them, Tobiah the Ammonite. At once Nehemiah concludes that their letters are full of malicious slanders about himself.*

Let not my reader imagine that I am siding with the Samaritans and their Jewish friends against Nehemiah. It is true, I think that the former had a right to feel aggrieved at the prospect of being deprived of their civil and religious privileges at Jerusalem, and that the Jewish conservatives were quite naturally drawn to the Samaritans among whom they found a sympathetic comprehension of their inherited prejudices. Some credit, too, is due in my opinion to the Jewish nobles for the assistance which they rendered to Nehemiah (whose ulterior object they did not perhaps see directly) in repairing the wall. But I think it quite possible that they painted Nehemiah too darkly in their private letters, and that they feed the prophet Shemaiah to induce Nehemiah to commit a questionable action. And Nehemiah's cause was a better one than theirs. An exclusive policy was necessary at this juncture in order that at a later day more catholic principles might become possible. Besides, the terms had, as it appears, been stated to the Samaritans on which their religious privileges could be continued to them, and these

* Neh. vi., 17-19. For "my words" read "evil reports of me."

terms they had rejected. They had even shown a loathing for the best Jewish piety (Isa. lxvi., 5), and, now that a capable leader of orthodoxy had appeared, they did their utmost to hinder his action. Surely this antagonism to what Nehemiah knew to be true righteousness might, from the governor's point of view, be plausibly regarded as obstinate wickedness, which deserved no courtesy or consideration.

To return to Nehemiah's personal history. The work for which he had obtained leave of absence from the court was finished. It is stated in our present text of the book of Nehemiah that he remained twelve years at Jerusalem as governor (Neh. v., 14). But without independent corroboration of this we must hesitate to accept it as correct. The Biblical texts underwent many changes, especially in points affecting chronology, before they reached the latest editors. The text of Neh. v., 14 can scarcely be accurate. Nehemiah must, it would seem, have gone back to Artaxerxes as soon as the work to which his firman referred was completed. The king had only given him leave for a set time, and the queen, too, was interested in his return. One pleasant thing however I have to mention which is beyond all doubt. Before his departure, Nehemiah showed a genuine sympathy with the down-trodden poor. The story of their " bitter cry " follows immediately on that of the building of the wall, and it was ultimately this great public work which caused the sad trouble of which they complained. For it was not possible that the poor Jews who laboured so continuously at the wall, should have time to attend to their fields and vineyards. The consequence was that the Persian tax-gatherer pressed them on the one hand, and Famine held them in his stern grip on the other. The only remedy was to apply to the money-lenders. But those harsh men would not be satisfied unless their clients mortgaged their small holdings, and even let their young sons and daughters go into slavery. "A great cry arose among the common people and their wives against their Jewish brethren." "We are of the same flesh as our brethren," they exclaimed in the anguish of their heart, "and our children have the same lineaments as theirs." The cry reached the governor in his palace, and passionate wrath seized him. He had not been prepared for this moral failure. He had hoped to find the Jews of Judæa not inferior in brotherly love to those of the Dispersion, who held it a sacred duty to redeem Jewish captives out of bondage. The idea of a rich Jew allowing a poor one to sell his child, and even buying the child himself, was abhorrent to Nehemiah. It was not only inhuman but irreligious, and the guilty act exposed the whole community to insulting taunts from the Samaritans. He called an assembly, and with dramatic gestures, which he has actually recorded, he made the usurers swear to cancel the mortgages, and remit the excessive interest which they had been exacting.

The story speaks badly for the religious life of the community. It reminds us of an anonymous prophecy written about this time, a specimen of which deserves to be quoted. The writer dramatically introduces the richer Jews expostulating with Jehovah on His inactivity as the protector of Israel.

"Why have we fasted, and thou seest it not? mortified ourselves, and thou markest it not?
Surely on your fast day ye pursue your business, and all money lent on pledge ye exact.
Is not this the fast that I choose, saith Jehovah,
To loose the fetters of injustice, to untie the bands of violence,
To set at liberty those who are crushed, to burst every yoke?
Is it not to break thy bread to the hungry, and to bring the homeless into thy house,
When thou seest the naked to cover him, and not to hide thyself from thine own flesh?
Then will thy light break forth as the dawn, thy wounds will be quickly healed over,
Thy redress will go before thee, and Jehovah's glory will be thy rearward.
Thy sons will build up the ancient ruins, thou wilt raise again the long-deserted foundations,

And men will call thee, Repairer of ruins, Restorer of destroyed places for inhabiting."
(Isa. lviii., 4, 6–8, 12.)

We see from this that Nehemiah was not the only person who revolted against the inhumanity of the aristocrats. Had he inquired, he would have found out this cruel conduct before. For it was not only the rebuilding of the walls which had given occasion to the usurers to torment the commonalty. He did not inquire, because he was too busy with high matters to look into small details. Nor had his kinsman Hanani warned him of the need which existed for a thorough social reform; Hanani was entirely absorbed in the idea of the necessity for ensuring religious isolation. And so Nehemiah, who also regarded this object as vital, drew these poor people from their country homes to labour on the wall without having made due provision for their compensation. Did he blame himself for this? He has unfortunately left no record in his autobiography.

Equally unrecorded are the rest of the acts of Nehemiah during his first visit. Possibly the later writer who edited his work has omitted some sections which did not fit into his own plan. Nor do we know the name and the religious tendency of the Tirshatha (*i. e.*, royal representative) to whom Nehemiah resigned the reigns of power. It is no great matter;

whoever the Tirshatha was, he had not the courage to cope with the Jewish aristocrats, who are found at a later time as intimate with the leaders of the Samaritans as if the wall had never been repaired. There was still a gulf between Babylonian and Judæan orthodoxy.

Can we doubt that this caused much dissatisfaction in the Jewries of Babylonia? or hesitate to connect it with the first great certain return of Jewish exiles to Palestine under Ezra the scribe? This great return would naturally be preceded by a journey of some of the leading Jews, including Ezra, to the Persian court with a petition for royal encouragement. And it is a fortunate circumstance that an authentic utterance of Ezra himself places this beyond all doubt, and enables us to infer the nature of his petition to Artaxerxes. These are the words to which I refer:—

"Blessed be Jehovah, the God of our fathers, who has put such a thing as this into the king's mind, to beautify Jehovah's temple at Jerusalem, and has caused me to find favour before the king and his counsellors and before all the king's mighty princes." (Ezr. vii., 27, 28.)

It appears then that the object of Ezra and his party was a distinctly religious one. It was not a mere national migration for which he desired the royal permission, but a grand attempt to prepare the way for the still delayed return of Jehovah to His land.

Nehemiah, Ezra, and Manasseh 55

To him, as to Haggai and Zechariah before him, a beautiful temple was a necessary condition of the restoration of Israel to the divine favour. The supposed firman, however, which is inserted before the words of Ezra which I have just quoted is much more precise in its expressions. It declares that Ezra the priest* and scribe is sent by the king and his counsellors to institute an inquiry into Judæan religion on the basis of the law which is in his hand. It even empowers Ezra to appoint magistrates and judges to judge the people of the province west of the Euphrates in accordance with this law, and should there be any who presume to disobey, or refuse to be taught, a strict sentence is to be passed upon them, ranging from simple imprisonment to confiscation of goods, banishment, and death.† This is all very strange. A violent interference with the religion of their Judæan subjects would have been a new departure in the policy of the Persian kings. Ezra makes no reference to any other object as approved by the king but that of the decoration of the temple. He also expressly says that he would not ask the king for a military escort, because he had said so much about divine providence (Ezr. viii., 22); this

---

* Some scholars doubt whether the priestly character of Ezra is historically certain.
† Ezr. vii., 11-26; cf. 2 Chron. xv., 13.

hardly looks as if he thought of pushing his reforms with the help of the government. That the firman is skilfully written, I should be the last to deny, but to defend it in its present form as a historical document, is beyond my ingenuity.* Nor am I at all sure that the date given in Ezra vii., 8, 9 is correct.

It is, however, quite certain that a considerable party of Babylonian Jews arrived at Jerusalem under Ezra. Indeed, the activity of Ezra, like that of Nehemiah, is absolutely necessary to explain the course of later Jewish history. But what he actually did cannot in all points be ascertained. The account transmitted by the Chronicler in the Books of Ezra and Nehemiah may be based on contemporary narratives, but contemporary narratives are not always strictly faithful. I know that I am touching the fringe of a troublesome question, but it is one which the student cannot evade considering, and on which I must tell him my own conclusion. No one likes to set aside the authority of an old document, but here it appears to me quite unavoidable. Whatever view we take of the meaning of the narrator, the story will not stand the tests of historical criticism. One

---

* On this and on the other problems of the careers of Ezra and Nehemiah, see special articles in Messrs. A. & C. Black's *Encyclopædia Biblica*, and *cf.* the translation of the Books of Ezra and Nehemiah (with notes) by Guthe in Prof. Haupt's *Bible*. See also Guthe's *History of Israel* (German).

possible view is that Ezra, on his arrival with firman and lawbook, found the former quite useless owing to the temper of the people, and waited thirteen years before he ventured publicly to introduce the latter. Others think that the narrator meant something quite different, viz., that Ezra did not think it important to feel his way and try his powers of persuasion, but at once introduced the law amidst the rejoicings of the multitude. I think myself that the latter view of the writer's meaning is the most natural one, but I find it not less difficult to accept as historical than the former. How, except by an appeal to force, Ezra can have won immediate acceptance for his lawbook, I do not understand. Did he make such an appeal, according to the document? No. The statement is that " all the people. . . . spoke to Ezra the scribe to bring the book of the Law of Moses which Jehovah had commanded Israel " (Neh. viii., 1), and that on the next day the heads of families joined the priests and Levites in a visit to the great legal expert, Ezra, to learn the orthodox mode of keeping the Feast of Booths. Now I do not deny that there was at this time a sincere attachment on the part of the leading Judæans to the older law, and I fully recognise the moral influence which must have been exerted by the new settlers from Babylonia, but I doubt whether a lawbook differing so widely from the older one (I will explain what Ezra's lawbook was presently), can have been at once accepted by the whole people and especially by the aristocratic class. True, the other view appears not less questionable. How can Ezra have waited thirteen years before he obeyed, and that most imperfectly, the plain command of Artaxerxes? I must confess, too, that the events which, according to the extant records, followed this supposed publication and solemn acceptance of the law confirm me in my sceptical attitude. I can partly understand the story of the introduction of the older lawbook under Josiah, but I cannot in the least comprehend the externally parallel narrative in Neh. viii. A small kernel of fact may not unreasonably be admitted. But the story, as it stands, is, I greatly fear, unhistorical.

Not less full of improbability is the story of the marriage-reforms in Ezra ix., x. Such a delicate matter as the alteration of marriage-customs cannot have been brought about so quickly and in such a rough-and-ready way. That the sight of Ezra, sitting with dishevelled hair in a stupor, and then the hearing of a solemn liturgical prayer, should have so unnerved the people who had married non-Jewish wives that they straightway volunteered to turn away their wives and their children, and that three days

Nehemiah, Ezra, and Manasseh 59

afterwards a still larger assembly should have gathered in cold rainy weather in the open air, and sanctioned the appointment of a commission to compel the offenders to carry out this resolution, is surely incredible. That there was anything like a general dismissal of non-Jewish wives and their children, not only psychological considerations, but certain important facts recorded in our documents* forbid us to believe.

Let no one suppose that I am trying to convert Ezra into a model of humanity. On the contrary, I think it likely that he was at first far too vehement in his language and rigorous in his demands, and I must express a fear that some too pliant persons may have given way to him. If these surmises are correct, the scribe Ezra was guilty of a distinct denial of the divine fatherhood—a doctrine expressed in the very first chapter of the narrative which introduces his lawbook. I am bound to denounce this as much as I sympathise with and admire the very different attitude of the apostle Paul. Nor can I help referring in this connection to the blessings which accrued to the English race through the union of a heathen king of Kent with a Christian princess from France. Gratitude for these blessings compels me to shrink with horror from the conduct of Ezra, if he gave

*See Ezr. x., 15 ; Neh. xiii., 23–27.

sufficient occasion for a narrative like that in Ezra ix., x.

And yet, even if Ezra was so far guilty, I must not ignore the existence of extenuating circumstances. This vehemence and rigour (so far as they are historical) were but the excess of his religious patriotism. They arose out of his dread of the too possible disastrous consequences of mixed marriages. A child is always affected permanently for good or for evil by the religion of its mother. There was a time when the religion of ancient Egypt became partly Semitic through the intermarriage of Egyptians and Syrians, and some of the least desirable religious peculiarities of the early Israelites were largely due to their intermarriage with the Canaanites. That was chiefly why Ezra and Nehemiah were so much opposed to mixed marriages. The religion which they desired to promote was a book-religion, which to a considerable extent recognised the claims of development; those of the Samaritans and the other small nations of Palestine were local, unprogressive religions, based on ancient custom. No doubt Ezra's policy was opposed to the doctrine of the divine fatherhood expressed in the first chapter of Genesis. But we can show from the Book of Malachi * that many of those with whom Ezra would

* Mal. ii., 10-16.

fain have dealt so barbarously had offered an equally flat contradiction to that great doctrine by turning adrift the Jewish wives whom they had married in their youth in order to marry foreign women. "Have we not all one Father? has not one God created us?" are the words in which Malachi indignantly reproves them. He also mentions the sad divisions in families which had arisen from these cruel divorces, the children having apparently taken the part of their disgraced mothers. And he seems to have painfully felt his own inability to reform this abuse, for he (or some not much later writer) has added this appendix to his prophecy,—

"Behold, I send you the prophet Elijah before Jehovah's great and terrible day come. He shall turn the hearts of the fathers to the children, and the hearts of the children to their fathers, lest I come and smite the land with a curse" (Mal. iv., 5, 6).

In other words, Malachi looked for a great religious reformer, who should make the people think of their family and social obligations, and of Jehovah's hatred for all un-Israelitish conduct. Jehovah had made no covenant except with Israel; those who formed an alliance of any kind, either with half-Jews like the Samaritans, or with non-Jews like the Philistines, Ammonites, and Moabites, and who, in order to do this, had put away their Jewish wives, provoked His displeasure. Such, too, we may presume was the theory of marriage inculcated by Ezra.

Very little, then, remains to the critical historian of the details of the story in Ezra ix., x. A somewhat more favourable judgment can, in my opinion, be passed on the account of the rise of the so-called congregation, or to borrow a more appropriate Greek term, the Ecclesia.* This narrative seems originally to have followed on that in Ezr. ix., x., the last words of which, as given in the true Septuagint text, are "and they dismissed them (*i. e.*, their foreign wives) with their children." It also undoubtedly presupposes that Ezra's lawbook had been generally accepted and was now in force. For it speaks of a long reading from the book of the law of Jehovah as having preceded the liturgical confession uttered by the Levites; the contents of the lawbook were something quite new to the audience. Now it is quite true that this cannot be the historical background of the formation of the congregation. The mixed marriages cannot to any great extent have been dissolved, and the lawbook of Ezra cannot have been generally or publicly accepted. But the scene in the foreground of the picture may still be correct. The Babylonian Jews who came up with Ezra certainly regarded themselves as the true Israelites, and it was

* *Cf.*, Hort, *The Christian Ecclesia* (1896).

only natural that they should form themselves into what claimed to be a national Ecclesia or assembly —the ideas of the church and the nation being henceforth inseparably fused together.* And to this assembly or congregation they would naturally admit, first, all who in the past evil days had protested against semi-heathenism, and who, in the words of Malachi (iii., 16), had "spoken often one to the other,"† and next, those who, under the influence of the new colonists, had given up their heretical customs, or, in the language of a contemporary,‡ had "turned from transgression in Jacob" (Isa. lix., 20). This congregation is the "Zion" of the later chapters of Isaiah, and its members are the "poor," the "meek," the "mourners in Zion," the "trembling listeners to Jehovah's word," of whom we read in late psalms, prophecies, and narratives.§ This congregation is also the feeble beginning of the great Jewish church, and the contract or covenant which its members, after a solemn reading of the new lawbook, probably subscribed, must have contained the

---

* According to the post-exilic list in Ezr. ii. (Neh. vii., 1 Esdr. v.), the number of men in the community was 42,360, *i. e.*, some 125,000 souls.

† *I. e.*, had formed themselves into a close association.

‡ See *Isaiah* in the *Polychrome Bible*.

§ Isa. lxi., 3; lxvi., 2; Ezr. ix., 4; x., 3; Ps. ix., 12, 18; x., 9, 10, 12, etc.

64 Jewish Religious Life after the Exile

chief obligations which were the condition of the privileges granted to the true Israel—privileges which are summed up in these remarkable words from the third part of Isaiah:

"And as for Me, this is My covenant with them, saith Jehovah: My spirit which is upon thee [*i. e.*, upon the true Israel], and My words which I have put into thy mouth, shall not remove from thy mouth, nor from that of thine offspring, nor from that of thine offspring's offspring, from henceforth unto eternity" (Isa. lix., 21).

At this historical turning-point the scribe, Ezra, suddenly disappears. The chief place in the narrative is once more occupied by Nehemiah, whom the news of Ezra's comparative failure seems to have drawn from his home in Susa.* Probably he came on furlough as temporary governor or special high commissioner. It is noticeable that even Nehemiah does not mention Ezra in the short second part of his memoirs. He confines himself to a business-like description of his own doings. He had three practical objects. They are the same which are given in the traditional account of the covenant of the congregation, viz., the abolition of mixed marriages, and of Sabbath traffic, and the provision of regular supplies for the temple services and for the priests and Levites.

* Neh. xiii. 6.

Nehemiah, Ezra, and Manasseh

Let us take the last of these points first: Nehemiah found that the support of the Levites had been so sadly neglected that they had deserted their posts and retired to their country allotments.* Strange to say, the priest Eliashib (I suppose he was the high priest of that name), acquiescing in the decadence of the ecclesiastical system, had conceded the use of a large store-chamber, formerly in the charge of the Levites, to Tobiah the Ammonite.† Here, perhaps, as the man of business of the temple, Tobiah had installed himself, with his household utensils, close to his priestly friend. Nehemiah, according to his wont, took prompt action. He cast out all Tobiah's property, and had the chamber purified, just as if Tobiah had been a heathen.‡ To Eliashib we are not told that he said anything, but to the civil rulers, who ought to have stirred up the people to bring their offerings, he gave a short but emphatic rebuke, "Why is the house of God forsaken"?§ The effect was immediate. The Levites were gathered together, and the arrears of tithe called in.∥ Thus this man of affairs, with his beneficently im-

---
* Neh. xiii., 10.
† Neh. xiii., 4, 5.
‡ Neh. xiii., 7–9.
§ These words have the ring of spontaneity. They are not taken from Neh. x., 39, but were evidently copied by the framer of the supposed covenant.
∥ Neh. xiii., 11, 12.

perious manner, succeeded where prophets like Malachi and priestly reformers like Ezra had failed.

It was a much harder task to get the Sabbath observed in the new orthodox fashion. Deuteronomy had only prescribed rest from the daily toil of husbandry; the priestly code required abstinence from all secular occupation, and represented even gathering sticks on the Sabbath as an offence deserving capital punishment.* Nehemiah, a partisan of this code, determined to press the later form of the Sabbath precept. He would trust no information, but, as on his first arrival at Jerusalem, went out to gather facts for himself.† It was a Sabbath-day, and the villages were enlivened with the merry shouts of those who trod the grapes in the wine-press, innocently supposing that this pleasant task was no violation of the Sabbath law. Then he looked elsewhere, and saw villagers lading their asses with grain, fruit, and wine, so as to arrive in Jerusalem on the next market-day. Nehemiah kept his counsel, but when the market-day came he warned the sellers not to start from home on the Sabbath-day again. The Sabbath trade in fish also excited his indignation, though he found fault not so much with the Tyrians who sold, as with the Jews who bought the fish.‡

---

* Num. xv., 32–36. † Neh. xiii., 15–22.
‡ It was salted and dried fish from the Mediterranean.

Nehemiah, Ezra, and Manasseh 67

Nehemiah administered a severe rebuke to the principal Jews, reminding them that Sabbath-breaking had brought ruin in the past, and that more troubles would be the consequence of such profane conduct. He gave orders that the city gates should be closed all through the Sabbath, and that no one bringing any merchandise should be admitted. The traders saw nothing for it but to pass the twenty-four hours of the Sabbath without the walls. But even this irritated the governor. The Jews who went out into the country on the Sabbath might be induced to attempt an infraction of the law. So Nehemiah threatened the traders that unless they desisted altogether, he would drive them from the neighbourhood by force.

It is a scene from real life which we have before us, and it helps us to understand the transition from the gentle code of Deuteronomy to the consistently severe code of Ezra. We have interesting utterances of men who sympathised with Nehemiah in what I may call the Nehemiah section of the Book of Isaiah—I refer, of course, to the well-known sayings on the Sabbath in Isa. lvi., 2, 6; lviii., 13. The passages are not fine enough to quote; in fact, the poetry of the Sabbath sentiment waited many centuries for a worthy expression.

And now comes the turn of the third great object

of the reformers, viz., the abolition of mixed marriages. Two noteworthy facts come before us. The first is Nehemiah's lenience to the common people, whom he did not compel to send away their Philistine, or Ammonite, or Moabite wives. With almost frantic excitement he made the offenders swear not to promote any more such marriages within their families, and there he stopped.* The second is his severity to the priests. A grandson of the high priest Eliashib had married a daughter of Sanballat. No doubt this is the Manasseh of whom, as I have already mentioned, Josephus tells us. Nehemiah himself relates that he made Jerusalem too hot for the offender, who fled precipitately. "Remember it is to them, and not to me," says Nehemiah, "that I have attainted priestly dignitaries." "On the other hand," he continues, "I have purged the priesthood from all strangers, and maintained each of the offices of the priests, and of the Levites." † From this we may infer that Manasseh had companions in his exile, and we have already seen that Nehemiah's view of his character is not the only one that is possible. Indeed, the governor himself brings no other charge against him but that of having criminally polluted a consecrated race. Manas-

* Neh. xiii., 23–27.
† Neh. xiii., 28–30 (new translation).

seh may have been a good, and was certainly in some sense a great, man. His reconstitution of the Samaritan community was an event of high importance in the history of Jewish religion.

Scanty enough are the record's of Nehemiah's second visit, but they suffice to show that his chief interest at this time was ecclesiastical. Perhaps he did not interfere with the civil government; this may have remained in the hands of the person whom he found in office. His main objects were those of Ezra, and it was his good fortune to succeed where the priestly scribe had failed, not merely because he had the royal authority, but because of his great personal qualities. Still, we must not allow ourselves to underrate Ezra. If the traditional picture of his activity is not fully historical, it devolves upon us to fill up the deficiencies of the narrative by reasonable conjecture. We must remember that Ezra was a theorist by education, and that he began his practical career with an imperfect knowledge of the situation. Under these circumstances it is intelligible that he was at first too vehement and arbitrary. But it is psychologically probable that when his first injudicious effort had failed, he showed himself in a more pleasing light. The portrait of the Servant of Jehovah, in some beautiful songs to which I shall refer, may not indeed have been sketched from Ezra, but seems to embody the ideal of the class to which Ezra belonged. I believe that his hidden life in the years which succeeded his public failure may have been great in the eyes of God. I believe that he must have come to understand how ill adapted the lawbook was in its original form to the wants of the Judæans, and that he devoted himself with considerate thoughtfulness to correcting some of its deficiencies. Henceforth he did not "cry, nor roar,* nor cause his voice to be heard in the street." With old and new friends he laboured to commend the claims of the reinterpreted law of Jehovah to the citizens of Jerusalem. And though I cannot venture to believe that he wrote psalms, I can imagine that he would have joined heartily in singing words like these:

> " Make Thy face to shine upon Thy servant,
> And teach me Thy statutes.
> Streams of water run down mine eyes
> Because men keep not Thy law."
>
> (Ps. cxix., 135, 136.)

There is yet another reason why Ezra should be had in honour, which rests probably on a firmer basis than the foregoing conjecture. In a document which is, at any rate, early—I mean the supposed firman of Artaxerxes (Ezr. vii., 12, 21)—he is

---

* See rendering of Isa. xlii., 2 (with note) in the *Polychrome Bible*.

described as the "writer of the law of the God of heaven," *i. e.*, of that law which Ezra brought with him to Jerusalem, and which the firman elsewhere calls "the law of thy God which is in thy hand." I believe that by this title the writer meant that Ezra was the author or editor of the lawbook referred to, for if "scribe" merely meant "copyist," what object would there be in giving Ezra the title? It would surely be no additional honour for a priest to be called a copyist. The firman indeed, cannot be regarded as an authority for the views of Artaxerxes, but the phrase "writer of the law of the God of heaven" (*i. e.*, of Jehovah) probably represents what Ezra said of himself when he came to Jerusalem. We are told that when, in Josiah's time, the Deuteronomic Law was brought before the secretary of state, Hilkiah the chief priest stated what he knew of the history of the document.* Ezra, too, was no doubt called upon to do this by the rulers of the Jerusalem-community, and he probably said that by the spirit of Jehovah he had reproduced the Law of Moses more perfectly than his predecessors.† A later writer, whose words are preserved in Ezr. vii., 6–10, was ignorant of this. He represents Ezra

---

* 2 Kings xxii., 8.
† Esdr. xiv., 44, is, of course, a wild fiction. For "204" read "94" (see Ball's *Variorum Apocrypha*).

as merely an experienced scholar in the law of Jehovah, who had devoted himself to teaching the divine statutes.

The lawbook of Ezra was no doubt a smaller work than what now passes among critics as the Priestly Code. Nor can we admit that it was altogether the work of Ezra. In the Babylonian, as well as in the early Persian period, different schools of priests appear to have occupied themselves with recombining, recasting, and supplementing the earlier laws and legal traditions. The state of Judæan religion about the middle of the fifth century made it plain that these labours needed to be brought to a provisional close, and it was probably Ezra who took the lead in the redaction of the material. It was his province, I suppose, to select, arrange, and complete the literary matter prepared by his fellow-priests.

You will now understand the sense in which I have spoken of Ezra's lawbook as new. It was new by comparison with Deuteronomy, just as Deuteronomy in its day (the time of Josiah) was new by comparison with the Book of the Covenant, which belonged perhaps to the time of Jehoshaphat. But it professed to hand on the old Mosaic laws and principles in a form adapted to the age of Ezra; and its profession was not unjustified. For it was perfectly clear to theists of that period that God had both the will and the power to endow chosen men with the spirit and capacity of Moses, just as, according to Malachi, he would at a future time endow a chosen prophet with the spirit and capacity of Elijah. I do not therefore mean by the phrase, a new lawbook, a book that was produced for the first time from the fertile brain of an enthusiast.

To understand Ezra's lawbook it is necessary to realise its object. This was not to cultivate a lofty type of personal piety, but to guard against a recurrence of the great national calamity of the past. The old religion of Israel, with all its attractive variety of local and family rites, had proved itself inadequate. The presence of the Divine King among His people had been continually interrupted. Tyrants had often usurped the dominion, for how could a God be said to rule in a conquered or even in a tributary land? and there had also been a permanent obscuration of the theocracy by the institution of a human royalty. Hence the necessity of a perfect divine law to which priests and laymen, rich and poor, should be equally subject—a law which should take into account the huge difference between God and man, and should spare no pains in determining the points in which a supernatural God would be necessarily offended—*i. e.*, in marking the limits between the holy and the unholy, the sacred and the profane. And since the primitive confusion of the material and the ethical was not yet overcome, and since it was vastly easier to deal with material than with ethical violations of the divine sanctity, it came to pass that the main subject of the Jewish, as well as of the Zoroastrian, law, was the distinction between clean and unclean, and the manner in which lost ceremonial purity could be recovered. It was only those who were technically clean who could appear before God, and the object of the elaborate sacrificial system was not to produce peace of mind for the individual, but to unify the community on a sound religious basis, maintaining its consecrated character unimpaired. The individual who voluntarily or involuntarily transgressed any precept of the law injured the sanctity of the community. As long, therefore, as his transgression was unatoned for, he was a source of danger to that organic whole of which he was a member. It mattered not whether the precept were moral or ritual; the divine holiness had been wronged, and satisfaction had to be given, either by ceremonial means or by the cutting off of the offending branch from the parent stem.*

---

* A punishment which, owing to the virtual abolition of the clan associations, placed him who suffered it in a truly terrible position.

Nehemiah, Ezra, and Manasseh 75

The most remarkable evidence that the legislation of Ezra's school was planned in the interest of the community, and not of the individual, is supplied by the rites of the Day of Atonement. The object of these was to clear away any impurity which the atoning acts of the past year might still have left in the community or in the sanctuary. They cannot however be shown to have existed as early as the time of Ezra, and probably are among the passages which are late insertions in the Levitical legislation.* One of the details of the ritual is so strange, and sheds so much light on the low spiritual state of the mass of the Jews, that I refer to it now. It has, in fact, strong affinities to customs mentioned by Mr. Frazer, author of *The Golden Bough*, as still prevalent in parts of India, Borneo, and other countries. The natives of these regions firmly believe that the demons who bring disasters and other calamities can be driven away by means of loud cries addressed to some quasi-sacrificial animal such as a goat, and we know from the Mishna that just such shouts, with just such an object, were addressed to the so-called scapegoat on the annual Day of Atonement. This unfortunate animal was driven into the wilderness bearing away all the sins committed by the Jews during the

---

* To some extent they were anticipated by a very simple ceremony enjoined by Ezekiel (Ezek. xlv., 10-20).

year, and the practice was to push it over a certain crag not far from Jerusalem, which has been identified, upon which it was received by Azazel, one of the fallen angels for whom this name, which is of quite a recent type, was invented.* Certainly this was a very strange concession to make to popular superstition, but it had this incidental advantage, that it counteracted the custom of sacrificing to goblins of the wilderness called " satyrs." † In fact, we must bear in mind that the Jews had not only hereditary superstitions of their own, but lived amidst a population still more superstitious than themselves, and that it was practically impossible, from a church-statesman's point of view, to avoid making some carefully guarded concessions to the weakness of human nature. Whether Ezra would have sanctioned so big a concession as that which relates to the scapegoat seems to me doubtful. And I think that there must have been many in the subsequent period who entertained a strong repugnance to the miserable ceremony of the scapegoat.

Another reason why it is of importance to realise the object of the lawbook, is this—that Protestant

---

* See article "Azazel" in Messrs. A. & C. Black's *Encyclopædia Biblica*.

† See "Satyrs" in the same *Encyclopædia*. Azazel may, as the present writer has suggested, have been substituted for some arch-goblin of Jewish folklore.

Nehemiah, Ezra, and Manasseh 77

students are naturally prone to criticise the legal religion from a Pauline point of view. Now Judaism as a whole is by no means devoid of spirituality, and has true saints of its own, but the Law from which it so largely springs cannot stand the tests which Pauline Christians apply to it. The Law may indeed encourage a deep awe of God, but this service can only be rendered to those who are already predisposed to such a habit of mind. I speak, of course, of the effect of the Law itself, and not as modified by the perusal of the prophetic Scriptures, and by the influence of the sweet hymns of the Psalter. And I regret that through unconsciously unfair criticism some injustice should be done to one of the most remarkable productions of the religious spirit.

There is yet another mistake against which we have to guard—that of supposing that Ezra's book was merely a lawbook. The legal element was indeed predominant, but the code was introduced, or accompanied, by a history of the origin of the sacred people and the sacred institutions. We are struck in this history by a diminished, though by no means extinct, regard for popular traditions, and an absence of the true historical interest. On the other hand, we are impressed by the deep religious earnestness of the writers, whose conception of God is higher and purer than that of the earlier narrators, and whose veneration for the sacred institutions is such that they declare one of them (the Sabbath) to have been ordained at the Creation, and another (Circumcision) to be as old as Abraham. The patriarchs, too, have put off the weaknesses with which early tradition had invested them. They are types of the perfect character after which each subject of the theocracy aspires, and their meritorious lives are among the palladia of the regenerate Israel.

It is true, there has been loss as well as gain. There is on the one hand a chilliness in the relation of the patriarchs to their God, and on the other an incomprehensibleness in the character of these saintly men, who strike a modern reader as having had no moral development. But this chilliness is by no means indifference; it is only the expression of feeling which is concerned. A priest is not a poet; it requires a poet to bring out the latent heat of Jewish religion in Ezra's period. And the incomprehensibleness of which I spoke is at once removed when we view Abraham, Isaac, and Jacob as types or ideals of the new Israel. For the new Israel was separated from the old by a deep gulf—the gulf of national ruin, over which the labours of Ezekiel, prophet and lawgiver, and his successors down to the time of Ezra had constructed a bridge. The bridge was the reinterpreted Law, but this bridge was only open to those who had taken to heart the lessons of the past. Such persons are the only true Israelites. They acknowledge that their old ideals and their old confidences were false, and they find new ones in the Law. Religion has transformed their views of character; it has also taught them to trust, not in chariots and horses, but in the strength vouchsafed to faithful obedience.* The only defect which an orthodox Jew could find in the life of Abraham was that he had no lawbook to study. But Job, who is, apart from some easily separable details, a poetical version of Abraham, shows by his grand profession of innocence (Job xxxi.) that all the essentials of the moral law were known to and observed by him in a spirit of devout obedience. The want of poetry in the priestly authors of the lawbook was supplied by later writers and not least by the poet of Job.

One thing, no doubt, Job lost for a time which the priestly writer makes extremely prominent in Abraham, and that is humility. Humility is the dominant note of the Jewish character as transformed by the Law. It is properly a relation to God, and it is the root out of which not only Israel's privileges but all its righteousness proceeds. Hence the re-

* *Cf*, the saying, " Everything is in need of help (from heaven)." Midrash on Ps. xx.

markable phenomenon that righteousness and humility in the post-exilic period are coupled together. "Behold, thy king comes to thee; he is righteous and victorious; humble is he, and he rides upon an ass" (Zech. ix., 9). And again, in a psalm, the wars of the Messiah are said to be waged "in behalf of truth, righteousness, and humility" (Ps. xlv., 4).

The one colossal privilege guaranteed in the future to the "humble" was the presence of God among His people, or, in other words, the visible assumption by Jehovah of His kingly dignity. When the priestly code was originally framed, it was hoped that this "great divine event" would speedily take place. This is why in Leviticus we so often hear the appeal, "Be ye holy, for I am holy" (Lev. xi., 44, etc). This, too, is the secret of all those minute prescriptions which strike most of us as wearisome, but which to those who had taken upon themselves "the yoke of the kingdom of heaven"[*] were delightful. The too early dimmed holiness of ancient Israel arose out of a preceding act of Jehovah (the Exodus); in the future, the delivering act of God would have to be preceded by a thorough sanctification of His people. This it was the endeavour of Ezra and his colleagues to secure, and judged from

---

[*] The phrase illustrates the saying of Jesus, "Take my yoke upon you, . . . for my yoke is easy."

their own point of view they did their work in the most self-denying and reverent manner.

For the number of ancient elements in the priestly legislation forbids us, as I have said, to call it in the strict sense of the word, a new, that is an entirely original, lawbook. It exhibits the form which the older legislation took under vastly altered circumstances, and it only differs so widely in many respects from that older legislation because of the great outward revolution through which Israel had passed, and which was resulting more slowly in an equally great change in the inner man. In that second revolution there were many other actors besides Ezra and the legalists. Priests, prophets, psalmists, and wise men, besides the humbler confessors of common life, all had their share in bringing about the transformation of Israel. To some of them it will be my privilege to call the reader's attention, but none of them deserves such high honour as Ezra the scribe, because without his lawbook the preliminary conditions of their activity would have been wanting. The Jewish and the Zoroastrian communities have survived centuries of persecution chiefly through their possession of a written religious Law. The known or unknown compilers of that Law are greater men than the founders of empires.

LECTURE III.

Jewish Religious Ideals; Hindrances to their Perfect Development.

THE Jewish community in Judæa had now been reconstituted. Come what might, it had a bond stronger than death linking it to the God of heaven and earth. True, it could not expect much prosperity in the immediate future. Ezra and Nehemiah must have known that a breathing-time between successive afflictions was all that could be hoped for.* But they knew also that they had provided the best of comforts for their afflicted people by stirring up within them a sense of the true Israelitish ideal. This ideal was not the same which had hovered before the minds of David and Solomon. It was not in the first place material prosperity, but simply to be and to do as a community all that

* This was one unfortunate result of the policy of Cyrus, who sought as much as possible to respect the individualities of the subject peoples. He meant well, but he did not foresee that these individualities would express themselves in a succession of revolts which it would be troublesome to his successors to quell. Not unfrequently these revolts took place in the neighbourhood of Judæa, and that small and poor country suffered many inconveniences in consequence.

Jewish Religious Ideals

a righteous God approved. A tender-hearted, zealous, and enthusiastic man placed his pen at the service of this ideal. He depicted some of its most beautiful aspects in a cycle of songs which some like-minded editor inserted at different points of the expanded prophecy of Restoration (*i. e.*, Isaiah xl.—lv.). Those who would comprehend the sanctified ambitions of some of the best Judæans in the age inaugurated by Ezra should read, and read again, these fine poems.

Let us begin with the poem which is most concrete in its expressions, and is most obviously occasioned by contemporary historical facts. I will give the central portion.* May the words find reverent and sympathetic readers.

" He grew up as a sapling before us,
And as a sprout from the root in a dry ground ;
He had no form nor majesty,
And no beauty that we should delight in him.

" Despised (was he) and forsaken of men,
A man of (many) pains, and acquainted with sickness ;
Yea, like one before whom men hide the face,—
Despised, and we esteemed him not.

" But our sickness (alone) he bore,
And our pains—he carried them,

---

* Isaiah liii., 2–9. This and the following translations from Isaiah are almost entirely from the *Polychrome Bible*, and are based on a text which differs in some points from that in common use.

Whilst we esteemed him stricken,
Smitten of God, and afflicted.

"But (alone) he was humiliated because of our rebellions,
(He alone was) crushed because of our iniquities;
A chastisement, all for our peace, was upon him,
And to us came healing through his stripes.

"All we, like sheep, had gone astray,
We had turned every one to his own way,
While Jehovah made to light upon him
The guilt of us all.

"He was treated with rigour—but he resigned himself,
And opened not his mouth,
Like a lamb that is led to the slaughter,
And like a sheep that before her shearers is dumb.

"Through an oppressive doom was he taken away,
And as for his fate, who thought thereon,—
That he had been cut off out of the land of the living,
(That) for my people's rebellion he had been stricken to death?

"And his grave was appointed with the rebellious,
And with the wicked his tomb,
Although he had done no injustice,
Nor was there deceit in his mouth."

How very natural was the question of the Ethiopian eunuch in the Acts, "Of whom, pray, does the prophet say this? of himself, or of some other man?" (Acts viii., 34). For this is obviously not a purely imaginary description, but a deeply felt meditation on certain melancholy facts well known to the poet and his readers. Supposing the poem to have been written at the end of the Exile, we might interpret it as a description of the persecution and death of the prophet Jeremiah, whom a plausible tradition declares to have been put to death by his unbelieving countrymen. It would seem, however, that the age of Ezra is a more defensible date, and in this case the facts to which the poet refers will probably * be the martyrdoms commemorated in a late prophecy of the Book of Isaiah (Isaiah lvii., 1) in these words:

" The righteous perishes, but no man lays it to heart ;
Men of piety are taken, but none considers
That for the wickedness (of the time) the righteous is taken."

It should not, I think, surprise us to find complaints like these in the years preceding the arrival of Ezra. Religious progress among the Jews was not obtained cost-free. Most of the Judæans in the first half of

* It is possible, however, that the traditional martyrdom of Jeremiah is referred to in a very late post-exilic prophecy as a great sin of the community. In Zech. xii., 10," they shall look (with longing regret) to me whom they pierced," cannot be right. It is just possible that "me" represents the first letter of "Jeremiah."

the fifth century were the children of those who had been left behind by Nebuchadrezzar, and were by no means faithful adherents of the Deuteronomic Law. Neither rich nor poor could stand a very strict scrutiny. Then, as afterwards, the rich were specially prone to sins of violence and inhumanity, while the poor were as much addicted to old and new superstitions. Exceptions, however, there certainly were. Malachi calls such persons "fearers of Jehovah," and intimates that they belonged to the poorer class. These poor but pious men appear to have been lightly esteemed by their neighbours, who ascribed their unprosperous and even miserable condition to the judgment of God, while the tyrannical rich men, to rid themselves of these troublesome nonconformists, sometimes accused them falsely before the judges, and obtained their condemnation to death. But that great religious thinker and poet of the age of Ezra to whom I have referred, looking back on these sad events, saw them irradiated by the light of a divine purpose. He fused the different nameless martyrs and confessors into a single colossal form,* and identified this ideal personage with the

---

* To call a people the servant of such and such a God is perfectly Semitic. Robertson Smith has quoted Arabic parallels, and passages like Deut. iv., 19; vi., 13; x., 12, 20, imply the same usage among the Israelites, though it was not apparently as common as the individualising application of the phrases.

true people of Israel. In doing so, he may very likely have thought of the prophet Jeremiah, who certainly regarded himself and his disciples as conjointly the sole representative of the true Israel.

Looking back, as I said, the poet saw the full preciousness of such a life, and divined the fragrance of its close in the eyes of God. This second Jeremiah could not be inferior to the first in religious insight, and must have known that his patiently borne sufferings would be more effectual than any of the legal sacrifices for the conversion and ultimate glorification of his people. In a converted and regenerate Israel he must have felt that all that was noblest in himself would live, and that so he would continue to work out the all-wise purposes of the one true God.

This wonderful poem, which is the holy of holies in the temple of the Old Testament, stands last in the cycle of the songs on the Servant of Jehovah. The three preceding poems describe the experiences of this great personage prior to his martyrdom, or rather, of those martyrs and confessors who had the special work of teaching and preaching. All who in any sense witnessed for Jehovah formed part of the true Israel—the "Servant of Jehovah," but there was a special appropriateness in applying the latter title to those who were engaged in pastoral and missionary work. In Isaiah xlii., 1-4, xlix., 1-6, and l., 4-9, the Servant of Jehovah is represented as an earnest and absorbed religious teacher, who is sometimes rewarded with success, but at other times meets with neglect or persecution. His work for Israel consists in "bringing back" the people to Jehovah's land, and the means by which he strives after this result is a skilfully varied eloquence, keen as a sword when close appeals to the conscience are needed (xlix., 1), but soft as milk when the weary and disconsolate have to be revived (l., 4; *cf.* xlii., 3). This implies first a persuasive exposition of the main principles of the Law, and next, for the benefit of the Jews of the Dispersion, a setting forth of the manifold blessings enjoyed by dwellers in the Holy City. It was indeed a great and noble mission, and the probability is that it would have satisfied the aspirations of the scribe Ezra.* But it did not satisfy the author of these poems, who had drunk in the spirit of more catholic teachers. Noble as the function was of re-establishing Jehovah's people, it was not quite the noblest, and so he represents the Servant of Jehovah as comforting himself for his slight success among the people of Israel with the thought of a still grander mission.

* It will be observed that not even the narrative introduction to Ezra's law-book contains any hint of the world-wide mission of the descendants of Abraham.

"And now, (thus) saith Jehovah,
He who formed me from the womb to be a Servant unto him,
That I might bring back Jacob unto him,
And that Israel might be gathered,—
It is too light a thing that thou shouldest raise up the tribes of Jacob,
And restore the preserved of Irsael;
So I set thee as a light of the nations,
That My deliverance may reach to the ends of the earth."

(Isa. xlix., 5, 6.)

It is the mission to the other nations which forms the theme of the very beautiful poem which opens the series of songs on the Servant. This time it is not the Servant who speaks, but Jehovah.

" Behold, My Servant, whom I uphold;
My chosen, in whom My soul delights;
I have put My spirit upon him,
He will set forth the law to the nations.

" He will not cry aloud, nor roar (as a lion),
Nor cause his voice to be heard in the street.
A cracked reed he will not break,
And a dimly burning wick he will not quench.

" Faithfully will he set forth the law;
He will not burn dimly nor despond,
Till he have set the law in the earth,
And for his instruction the far countries wait."

(Isa. xlii., 1-4.)

Can there be a finer description of the true missionary? He is not allowed to abate one jot of the legitimate demands of truth, which is no mere theory to him, but a law, but he is to lay the chief stress on the capacity of that law to satisfy the deepest wants of human nature, bringing strength to the "cracked reed" and light to the "dimly burning wick." Persuasion, not force, is to be the instrument: how unlike the method ascribed, with some exaggeration, to Ezra!

And who is this model pastor and missionary? Is he a historical individual who has escaped mention in the hagiology of Judaism? No. In the first three songs the Servant is still an imaginative fusion of many individuals, and the persons who are here combined into an organic whole are the noble teachers and preachers of the Jewish religion in and after the time of Ezra. These the poet evidently supposes to form a numerous band, for, in order to realise his description, some will have to go to Babylonia, others to Egypt, and others to the Mediterranean coast-lands on their apostolic mission. Nor is there anything surprising in this. The prophetic and missionary view of Judaism is repeatedly brought before us in the later Scriptures (see Lecture VI.), and must have taken its rise in some highly gifted and illumined intellect. I can hardly think that the

Book of Jonah supplies us with the right starting-point. The idea of the missionary prophet Jonah, who is also a symbol of Israel, must surely have been suggested by some work in which the same idea was more directly expressed.

But is this really the idea of the songs of which we are now speaking? Certainly. These earnest teachers of the Law at home and abroad—who are they but the apostles or messengers of a great central body—the Jewish congregation formed by Ezra? It may be specially the teachers who say, "I have laboured (as it seems) for naught, but my recompense is with my God," yet it is the whole of faithful Israel which will share the reward promised in Isaiah lii., 13-15. Without the support of the congregation what would the teachers be able to effect? "All the congregation," as the Priestly Record says, "are holy, and Jehovah is among them" (Num. xvi., 3), and it was the aspiration of Zion that all her sons might be "disciples of Jehovah" (Isa. liv., 13), and that all Jehovah's people might be prophets (Num. xi., 29). Some might be called to a life of pastoral activity; others might simply have to witness to the truth by "doing justly, loving mercy, and walking humbly with their God" (Mic. vi., 8). Both modes of life were equally fitting and necessary, if that high utterance, "I will form thee and make thee a covenant for the people,* a light of the nations " (Isa. xlii., 6), was to be verified.

The insertion of these songs was the second enrichment which the original Restoration-Prophecy experienced. It is manifest that it greatly increased the influence of the prophecy. For, when a fresh appendix to this work in its expanded form was thought of, the writer at three points introduced the Servant of Jehovah soliloquising.† Here, however, the Servant is evidently regarded as a personification of the company of prophets, to which, of course, the writer himself belongs. The prophecy opens with these inspiring words, which so finely express the prophetic ideals of the time:

"The spirit of the Lord Jehovah is upon me, because Jehovah has anointed me, and has sent me to bring good news to the afflicted, to bind up the broken-hearted, to proclaim liberty to the captives, and opening of the eyes to the blind, to proclaim Jehovah's year of favour, and the day of vengeance of our God, to comfort all mourners, to give them instead of ashes a coronal, oil of joy for the garment of mourning, a song of praise for a failing spirit." (Isa. lxi., 1–3.)

A psalmist, too, was kindled to enthusiasm by the

---

* "A covenant for the people," because the Servant of Jehovah, who so thoroughly knows His will and is empowered to carry it out, is like an embodiment of His promise or agreement (*bĕrith*). *Cf.* 2 Cor. iii., 2, "Ye are our epistle."

† Isa. lxi., 1–3; lxii., 1, 6–7. See *Polychrome Bible.*

songs on the Servant of Jehovah. He lived in one
of those dark periods which succeeded the governor-
ship of Nehemiah, and which have left their impress
on so many of the lyrics in the first Book of the
Psalter. He is the author of the first part of Psalm
xxii., to which, as it seems, a conclusion has been appended by another hand. Into the poetical and
spiritual beauties of this fine fragment, I will not
enter. Suffice it to say that they could never have
existed but for that mine of poetry and religion—
the Book of the Second Isaiah in its expanded form,
and that chief among the spiritual beauties is the
energy with which the writer expresses the solidarity
of all true Israelites. The Servant of Jehovah, as
he at least understands the phrase, is certainly not a
guild or company of prophets, but the whole congregation of faithful Jews in Judæa. And hence
one notable difference between this psalm-fragment
and Isaiah liii., viz., that, while in the latter poem
the Servant of Jehovah suffers with full consciousness of the object and issue of his troubles, in the
former, God seems to have given over to death His
servant, who, nevertheless, refuses to forsake his God.
In short, Psalm xxii. presents us with a perfectly
new phase of Jewish religious thought. Before, the
Exile men forsook their God when He proved unable
or unwilling to protect them. But the congregation

of faithful Israelites which was founded by Ezra was able to trust its Father and its God even in the dark.

I now pass on to another form of the Israelitish ideal—that which centres in the person of the Messiah. The origin of the Messianic hope among the Jews is unrecorded. The first glowing expressions of it are in Isaiah ix., 2–7, and xi., 1–8. Both these passages are most probably post-exilic, and of a not very early date in the post-exilic period. It would seem as if the idea only gradually took hold of the religious leaders. Ezekiel had it for a time (see Ezekiel xvii., 22–24), but virtually abandoned it. For, though he nominally includes the figure of a second David in his later eschatological picture,* yet he deprives this David of all that in the olden time made the life of a king desirable. He permits him no freedom of movement, and practically condemns him to be simply the foster-father of the Church, with the duty of providing the external requisites of the temple ritual. King he will not call him; the second David is only to be a chief or prince. I suspect, however, that Ezekiel went too far for many of his readers. The popular Messianic hope could not be put down by a single great teacher. There was a deeply rooted belief that a day was at hand when the lots of the oppressors and the oppressed would

* Ezek. xxxiv., 23, 24 ; xxxvii., 24, 25.

be reversed. And, however true it might be that Jehovah was the Goël,—the deliverer of Israel,—a king who governed, as well as reigned, seemed to most Jews indispensable as the apex of society. It was only a few like Ezekiel who could rise to the thought of a church-nation, of a people entirely absorbed in religion, whose meat and drink it was to do Jehovah's will. And so we find the works of Isaiah and Jeremiah interspersed, through the labours of editors who were no mere literary craftsmen, but knew the people and their spiritual cravings, with what may in various degrees of strictness be called Messianic prophecies.

One of these produced a really remarkable effect. We have it in two forms. Neither of them is quite correct. But if we take the best readings from each we get this version of the prophecy, which, not without due recognition of what may be said on the other side, I incline to ascribe, not to Jeremiah himself, but to a member of the school of that prophet:

"Behold, the days come, saith Jehovah, when I will raise up to David a sprout of the right kind; he will reign as a king, and will deal wisely, and execute justice and righteousness in the land. In his days Judah will be delivered, and Jerusalem will dwell securely; and this is the name which will be given her—Jehovah is our righteousness."* (Jer. xxiii., 5, 6; xxxiii., 14-16.)

* Comp. the name of Jerusalem at the end of Ezekiel (Ezek. xlviii., 35).

Well did an editor of Jeremiah describe this saying as "that good word which Jehovah has spoken" (Jer. xxxiii., 14). It may have been the earliest written word of the kind, and certainly it had increased effect through being ascribed to Jeremiah. Did the prophetic writer really mean to attach his hopes, for better or worse, to the Davidic family? or did both he and Ezekiel use "David" as a symbolic term for an ideal ruler? The question has already been raised in connection with an episode in the life of Nehemiah. I am inclined to think that the prophet would not have cared to answer it. In fact, the event alone could prove who was the destined Messiah, and when it appeared to be Jehovah's will not to fulfil His "faithful oath unto David" (Ps. cxxxii., 11) in the person of a chosen Israelite, a deep silence must for a time have fallen on the Messiah's prophets. The author of the songs on the Servant of Jehovah refers to no Messianic king; indeed, he goes so far as to use expressions conventionally appropriated to a Messianic conqueror in a new, metaphorical sense. He says that the Servant of Jehovah, the true or spiritual Israel, shall have a portion allotted him with the great, and shall divide spoil with the strong (Isa. liii., 12); and in the same spirit the author of the first appendix to the Restoration-Prophecy makes Jehovah say to the people of Zion:

"I will make an everlasting covenant with you,
The sure promise of loving-kindness to David";

and he adds that, as in the olden time at the call of David, so now at the call of Israel the peoples shall hasten to incorporate themselves in the Israelitish empire (Isa. lv., 3-5). In other words, the idea of personal royalty has for these religious thinkers lost actuality; each Israelite is a prince, and the collective church-nation is Jehovah's anointed.

The currents of thought, however, at this time were changeable, and we must not be surprised to find the flame of the Messianic hope burning up again. Jeremiah was no doubt believed to have sanctioned it, and the posthumous influence of this prophet was great. It is to this period that we cannot help assigning some of the Messianic passages now extant in the Books of Isaiah and Micah. No historian of the phases of early Jewish religion could ignore these; some of them at least are inshrined, and deserve to be inshrined, in our memories and in our hearts. We may not pin our hopes to them in their literal meaning, but their vague magnificence encourages a higher and a larger application.

The prophetic poems in Isaiah ix., 2-7, and xi., 1-8, occur at the close of two collections of prophecies of Isaiah in which reference is made to a sore judgment upon Jerusalem.

To adapt these somewhat disheartening works to post-exilic use an editor appended two new prophetic passages breathing the spirit of the much-read consolatory prophecies of Jeremiah and the Second Isaiah. It appears as if all the ancient prophecies were felt to require such adaptation. The literary value of the inserted matter varies considerably, but the prophecy of the " King of the Four Names "* is a work of no slight significance. Let me endeavour to describe it.

It is a prophecy of comfort, addressed to those who deeply need it. Prophets of the old style were rather censors than comforters; their spirit is expressed in those words of Amos, " Can a trumpet be blown in a city, and the people not be afraid?" (Amos iii., 6). But our prophet belongs to the company whose beneficent program is so finely described in the words of Isaiah lxi., " He has sent me to bind up the brokenhearted," and who prefer the flute to the trumpet. Our prophet is as tender and sympathetic as the angel of the Lord in those exquisite narratives which open the third of our Gospels. He knows, of course, that Israel has sinned, but he knows, too, that the taskmaster has exceeded the limits of his commission. So one night, when neither moon nor stars are shining, he goes forth. He guesses rather than sees how early

* So Prof. G. A. Smith.

travellers are stumbling on the dark mountains, and anxiously looks for the first streaks of dawn. Suddenly the scene is transformed. Far more quickly than the music changes in the chorus of Handel's *Messiah* the gloom disappears. The sun leaps up from the horizon; "the people that walked in darkness have seen a great light." It is a spectacle such as may be seen in Palestine any summer's morning. But this time something warns the seer that there is a sacramental meaning in it. It is a pledge of the long-looked-for deliverance, an unspoken prophecy from the Eternal. Henceforth he will wait in the patience of hope, for the fulfilment "will surely come, it will not tarry." He can almost welcome the deepening shades in the last century of the Persian rule, for, as in the olden time, it is at midnight that the divine Redeemer will appear. The deliverance will be Jehovah's, but the work which follows the deliverance will be the Messiah's. The prophet, if I should not rather say the poet, remembers the old prophecy of Immanuel, whom he takes to be the Messiah,* and from a study of the whole collection of prophecies, to which he is providing an appendix, he concludes that, when the oppressor (*i. e.*, the Persian rule) is put down, the Messiah will be of an age to take upon himself the burden of government.

* On the probably true meaning of Immanuel, see *Polychrome Bible* (English and Hebrew editions).

"For a child has been born to us, a son has been given to us,
And dominion is laid upon his shoulder;
His name is Counsellor of Wonders,
Strong divine being, father of glory,* prince of peace.
Dominion is increased, and to peace there is no end,
On the throne of David, and throughout his kingdom,
To establish and support it by justice and righteousness
From henceforth to eternity; Jehovah's zeal will perform this." (Isa. ix., 6–7.)

Such is one of the current ideals of Israel's restoration. Society is to culminate in a potent and invincible but also peace-loving king, something like the Nebuchadrezzar of the Babylonian inscriptions. His empire, however, is to be much smaller than Nebuchadrezzar's. At any rate our poet is only interested in the restoration of a kingdom not less extensive than that ascribed to David. We find a similar expectation in the post-exilic appendix to Amos (ix., 11–12), but it is not expressed with the fervour and rhythmic beauty which are so admirable in the poem now before us.

And yet, if we can only resist the glamour with which early associations have invested this poem, we must confess that it cannot for a moment compare with the description of the Servant of Jehovah in Isaiah liii.; its ethical arc of more significance than

* *I. e.*, glorious father of the family of Israel.

its religious contents. The author of the latter has, in the most essential respects, passed beyond the ideal of a personal Messiah, though he still feels a tenderness towards it, and perhaps hopes by adopting some spiritualised features from it to win acceptance for his own nobler vision. It was a step which the greatest subsequent teachers could not retrace—a step which, quite independently, the early Buddhists took, when they identified the lowly Buddha with the righteous and mighty king who lived in the popular hopes—a step which the disciples of Jesus could not be prevented from taking afresh, and which the course of providential education has rendered harmless. For, as Professor Rhys-Davids has well said, " the Christian Messiah is as much higher and more noble than the previous conception of the first-century Jews, as the Buddhist King of Righteousness is higher and more noble than the previous Hindu conception of the King of Kings." *

The second of the two Messianic insertions is that which begins :

" And a rod shall come forth out of the stock of Jesse,
And a shoot shall grow out of its roots." †

It is very possibly by the same writer as the first portrait, which closes, as you remember, with a

* *Hibbert Lectures for 1881*, p. 136. † Isa. xi., 1.

reference to the king's justice and righteousness. It is not indeed in the same rhythm, nor is it so suffused with emotion. But the new rhythm and the new tone may have seemed to suit the new subject better. And I think we may detect the same moderation in the description of the Messiah which we found in the first portrait—a moderation which may fairly be ascribed to the influence of Isaiah. For I confess I cannot help believing that both these poetical descriptions were written to supplement the second and third prophetic collections of Isaiah respectively.* And certainly one of the germs of both passages is to be found in the saying of Isaiah, "And I will bring back thy judges as at the first, and thy counsellors as at the beginning; thereafter thou wilt be called, Citadel of righteousness, faithful city" (Isa. i., 26).

The whole prophecy or poem is most interesting. It is one of those dreams which feed the world with moral energy, and it reflects honour on the circles from which it proceeded. It is, however, a severe satire on the kings of past history, which, perhaps, accounts for the fact that the new king is called, not a son of David, but a son of Jesse. The person of

---

* This may account for the singular fact that the writer of Isa. xi., 1-8, uses neither the verb "to sprout" nor the noun "sprout." These words would have suggested the influence of Jer. xxiii., 5.

Jewish Religious Ideals 103

the Messiah is indeed encompassed with mystery. Somewhere doubtless he exists, all unconscious of his future greatness, but not till the right moment has come will the divine gifts qualifying him for his office descend upon him. Then will that saying of a late prophet be verified—that the house of David will be "as God" (Zech. xii., 8); the ideal king will be a divinity not only in might but in wisdom. As a judge, he will see the truth and the right at once, and his judicial energy will enable him to extirpate the first shoots of evil.* A limited ideal, some of us may think. But be sure that the poet means more than he says. For what does he tell us next? Like Virgil † in the Messianic Eclogue, he sings of the wolf dwelling with the lamb, and the leopard lying down with the kid. ‡ This is no mere allegory. It means that peace will one day prevail throughout the animal world. But can this be all? To what purpose would this feature in the description be unless it implied the extinction of the wolf-like element in human nature? Certainly it does imply this; and consequently this Messianic portrait also implies

* " With the breath of his lips he will slay the wicked " (Isa. xi., 4).
† In the cathedral of Zamora in Spain, Virgil is represented among the Hebrew prophets.
‡ In a great Indian epic it is said that " weasels sport with serpents, and tigers with deer, through the power of saints of brilliant austerity " (*Mahabhārata*, quoted by Muir, *Ancient Sanscrit Texts*, iv. 158).

an organised system of moral and religious instruction. For though the Messiah might put down the wicked oppressors by violence, he could never induce a tyrant to assume the meekness of a lamb. Jehovah no doubt is the great teacher. But prophets, moralists, and expounders of the Law are His deputies, and our far-seeing prophetic writer presupposes their activity as a condition of the ideal future.

But, before entering farther into this attractive subject, we must examine some other expressions of the hope of the Messiah. For these we naturally turn to the Psalter, which, being a congregational handbook, may be expected to refer to such a popular belief. What we find, however, is somewhat surprising. The temple poets went so far as to indite psalms which presuppose that a Davidic king, strong, warlike, and righteous, is already seated on the throne. Probably the psalmists before the Exile had accustomed the Israelites to the use of psalms in honour of the reigning king, and the newer psalmists would not abandon the custom, which, moreover, enabled them to give a striking expression to the burning faith in God which possessed them. Of a glorious future in store for the church-nation they were as much convinced as of their own existence. Whenever they prayed for it, an inner voice assured them that the answer was on its way; all that they had to do was to wait in hope. This accounts, not only for the abrupt alternation of intense supplication and exultant thanksgiving in many psalms, but for the strange addresses to an as yet non-existent king. I must confess that this impairs the claim of the psalms to lyric naturalness. Any interpreter approaching the so-called royal psalms for the first time would suppose them to refer to a contemporary historical king. Appearances are very strongly in favour of this view, which at once makes the psalms fresh and interesting even to a non-religious reader, and yet appearances are here for the most part illusory. Truth is truth, and even when it makes against some one of our most cherished desires—such, for instance, as the development of a stronger literary interest in the Psalter,—we must accept it with cordiality.

I venture, therefore, to state my opinion that it is only in the latter part of the Psalter that we can safely hold that a historical sovereign is spoken of, and that in the two psalms which have to be thus explained (viz., ci. and cx.) loyal followers have so idealised their prince that a Messianic reference must very soon have been thought of. The probable omission of the latter part of Psalm cx. may have arisen from a desire to facilitate such a reference. I would gladly pause for a few minutes on each of these psalms. For, however short, they are exceedingly interesting when read in the light of early Maccabæan times, and tell us things which we should not have known, or at least should not have realised, from the pages of history. But their religious contents are meagre. The Second Psalm throws more light on the Messianic belief; the Fifteenth and Twenty-fourth shed more on the best Jewish morality.

We pass on to the unexpected phenomena which await us. Two of the strangest Messianic psalms are the Twentieth and the Twenty-first.* Both relate to the Messianic king, who is supposed to be on the throne. In the former he is represented as just starting to fight with the enemies of Israel. It is perhaps his first campaign, for in Psalm xxi. the church-nation, in praising God for the king's victory, represents the total destruction of the enemies as still future. But even stranger is the Forty-fifth. The Messiah (who is modelled on the idealised Solomon) has come to the throne. To complete his happiness and to continue his line he is about to contract a marriage with a "king's daughter," or rather "royal maiden" (v. 13). The psalm is an

* Both these psalms have numerous points of contact with undeniable post-exilic psalms (see Cheyne, *Origin of the Psalter*). To interpret them with reference to a pre-exilic king is therefore not advisable.

encomium on the royal pair, who are supposed to have just met. The imaginative licence of the poet is great. But he does not lose his hold on the main object of the Messiah's existence, which is not mere private happiness, but the conferring of benefits on the church-nation.

> "Gird thy sword on thy thigh, O hero,
> Put on thy glory and thy state.
> He leads thee, and makes thy course to prosper,
> In behalf of truth, righteousness, and humility;
> Terribly will his right hand conduct thee,
> While peoples fall prostrate beneath thee." *
> (Ps. xlv., 3, 4.)

From a moral point of view this deserves special attention. Here is a victorious king whose achievements are not for himself, but, like those of Arthur in the great moralised legend of Tennyson, "in behalf of truth, righteousness, and humility," just those qualities, be it remarked, which pious Jews sometimes feared were perishing out of the earth. I think I ought to add that an approach to this conception is made by Nabopolassar, Nebuchadrezzar, and Neriglissar, kings of the later Babylonian Empire, each of whom gives himself the novel epithet of "humble." †

* The translation here, as elsewhere, is taken from the forthcoming second edition of a work on the Psalms by the present writer.
† Schrader's series of translations from cuneiform texts, iii., 2, pp. 3, 7, 77.

Another Messianic psalm, the Seventy-second, which is in fact the supplement of the Forty-fifth, gives just the same character to the ideal king, only it does not draw out the striking contrast between the martial prowess and the inward humility of the king—a contrast which, as you will remember, a famous Messianic prophecy in the Book of Zechariah (ix., 9) puts very forcibly. What the Seventy-second Psalm says (vv. 13, 14) is this:

> "He feels for the wretched and needy,
> The souls of the needy he delivers;
> From violence he redeems their souls,
> Yea, costly is their blood in his sight";

i. e., not as a matter of mere duty, but from sympathy, he places his strong arm at the service of those who are in need. Instead of despising the poor, he regards their blood as something too precious to be squandered.

I must not linger on this interesting poem. But I may point out the strangeness of the opening couplet, where the Messiah is represented as not only a king but a "king's son." This agrees with a passage in Psalm xlv. in which the "fathers," *i. e.*, the royal fathers, of the Messiah are spoken of. The psalmists leap over the interval between the last king of Judah and the accession of the Messiah, and represent the latter as the son of all the kings who have gone before.

The truth is that the Messiah is but a poetic embodiment of the Davidic royalty, and the Davidic royalty, in the absence of any real political interest, is but a representative of the Jewish people.* In the ideal democracy, each citizen is a king; in the idealised Jewish state, each true servant of Jehovah is as holy as the Messiah. This accounts for the striking fact that in the Eighty-ninth Psalm the people of Israel actually assumes the title of Jehovah's anointed.† Let me now direct your attention to this psalm, or at least to verses 19-51, which seem originally to have had a separate existence. This passage begins with a poetic version of a prophecy which attracted much attention in the Persian period—the "prophecy of Nathan" in 2 Samuel vii.:

> "My covenant I will not profane,
> Nor alter that which has passed My lips;
> Once for all have I sworn by My holiness,
> I will never be faithless to David.
>
> "His offspring shall endure for ever,
> And his throne as the sun before Me;

---

* Here we are constrained to differ from R. H. Hutton, where he says so finely (*Essays*, i., 274) that the Jewish prophets began to learn that "there must be, *between* the Father and human nature, some being lowly as the latter, perfect as the former, whose kingliness would not consist in mere righteous power, but in righteous humility." Righteous humility and nearness to God are as characteristic of the people as of its ideal ruler and representative.

† *Cf.* the same phenomenon in Ps. xxviii., 7, lxxxiv., 10; Hab. iii., 13.

> It shall be established for ever, as the moon,
> (Yea,) be steadfast as the meeting-place in the sky."

The "meeting-place in the sky" (if the words are rightly so read) is the "mountain of assembly," where, according to an old myth, the "sons of God" (or supernatural beings) spoken of in Job met together; whose top reached to the sky, and whose foundation was in the ocean which encompasses the earth. What better image of security could there be?* But the psalmist, after quoting the prophecy, falls into deep depression. He complains that the prophetic promise is in violent contrast to facts. The royalty of David's house is at an end, and the people of Israel, here identified with the Messiah, is treated with worse than contempt by its neighbours.

The Eighteenth Psalm is not less paradoxical. I am afraid that it has sometimes been admired on wrong grounds. It will not do to compare it to the splendid triumphal ode addressed to Thutmes III., King of Egypt, the language of which is as vivid and spontaneous as that of the Eighteenth Psalm is pale and artificial. To appreciate the latter we must read it as the expression of that "other-worldly" temper which no people has ever possessed as fully as the Jewish. From the very first the psalmist transports

---

* Precisely such an image is used by Ezekiel (xxviii., 13, 14) to express the self-confidence of the king of Tyre.

us to the Messianic age. The judgment on the nations has taken place*; Israel, with a Davidic king at its head, has been raised to the height of prosperity. It is this Davidic king who speaks in the psalm. He has no private ambitions, and can therefore interpret the thoughts of the community; indeed, the psalmist sometimes forgets the king, and speaks for the personified people.† All this is psychologically most strange. If it were not susceptible of the strictest proof, we should never have believed it possible.

A similar explanation must be given of the Second Psalm. Like the Eighteenth it is an attempt at a vivid realisation of the more strictly Messianic prophecies. In the Eighteenth Psalm, the Messianic king speaks as if he were on the throne, and, under Jehovah, controlled the destinies of the nations. In the Second, he speaks as if the confederate kings were planning a revolt from Jehovah and His anointed. There is less human nature in the Messiah who speaks here than in the portrait of him in the twin psalm. There, the work given him to do made a strong demand on his energy; he needed (as all the great religious Oriental conquerors felt that

* Ps. xviii., 4-19; *cf.* xcvii., 1-6.
† Hence in Ps. cxliv., 1-11, a highly imitative work, the words of Ps. xviii. are plainly adopted by the personified community, which frankly distinguishes itself from David.

they needed) a power which came from above to make the effort. Here, he has but to lift his sceptre of iron to shiver the nations like potters' ware. Morally the psalmist stands higher than his hero. He does not wish evil to the kings of the earth. The Messianic king cannot take steps against them till Jehovah's anger is kindled. Till then there is time for the kings to repent, and to renew their homage.

> " Now therefore, ye kings, show your wisdom ;
> Take warning, ye judges of the earth.
> Serve Jehovah with fear,
> And do homage with trembling,
> * Lest He be angry, and your course end in ruin.
> For soon His anger kindles ;
> Happy all those that take refuge in Him."
> (Ps. ii., 10–12.)

One reflection, I am afraid, will be forced upon you—that, if it is a benefit to the nations to be brought under the yoke of the Messiah, the benefit is one which requires of them the most painful sacrifices. The sternness of the foreign policy ascribed to the Messiah cannot, as we should say, be morally justified except on the theory that the nations are

---

* Here the ordinary versions insert " Kiss the Son," which, however, is due to a misunderstanding. " Kiss," *i. e.*, " do homage," should certainly be substituted for " Rejoice " (see the common version) in the preceding line ; " the Son " is a supposed translation of what is really a fragment of the word rendered " with trembling." (See the writer's *Book of Psalms*, 2d ed.)

thoroughly bad, and that their continued independence endangers the highest human ideals. This was, in fact, the belief of pious Jews whenever there was much friction between them and their rulers, and it expressed itself more particularly in the lyrics which they chanted in the temple. We shall see, however, that the psalmists do not always speak of the nations outside in the same hard tone. Nor do the prophetic writers. But we must, I think, earn the right to luxuriate in the gentler passages by first realising, under the guidance of the psalmists, the terrible state of tension in which the Jews too often lived.

I am aware that an eminent Jewish writer (Isidore Loeb) has denied the objective accuracy of the psalmists; he regards the Psalter as merely a picture of peculiar and abnormal states of mind. According to him, the psalmists are idealistic poets, who have discovered the art of turning their misery to the best account, and who find the taste of sorrow not wholly bitter. They are the dupes and sports of their imagination; they live in dreams, and have no sentiment of reality. There is some truth in this, but not very much. Like the prophets, the psalmists have a tendency to exaggeration. Their feelings are so intense that they cannot help laying on the colours too thickly. They love the ideals committed to them so well that they cannot be quite fair to those who would trample those ideals in the dust. And there is certainly a sweetness in their sufferings which an outsider cannot understand; for, the more miserable they are, the more they realise that one stronger than the strong cares for them. Nor are they altogether without some faint idea of the consolations of art, though the art may be of a kind which baffles our comprehension—I mean the music and singing of the temple. Certainly their one great pleasure is singing the praises of Jehovah. The mere recollection of this is a comfort to them in exile. One of the psalmists, when far from Zion, finely says:

" This do I call to mind, pouring out the while my languid soul,
 How I moved in converse with the noble to the house of God,
 Amid the sound of praiseful song, the music of those who kept the feast." (Ps. xlii., 4.)

It may further be admitted that the pious were to some extent the authors of their own misery. They had no political insight, and were incapable of practical compromise; they had also an absolute distaste for commerce, and were strangers to the arts of the market-place. The result was that both politically and commercially they were pushed to the wall, not only by foreigners but by men of their own race.

It was this indeed which made their feelings so bitter—that men who called themselves Jews should associate with the heathen and adopt their worldly principles—that all the zeal and energy of Nehemiah and Ezra should have failed to realise the noble ideal of the church-nation. That the non-Jewish and half-Jewish populations of Palestine should show irritation at the religious assumptions of the Jews, was only to be expected; that the Persian rulers should grow tired of the friendly indulgence of Cyrus and Darius was at any rate not quite unintelligible; but that members of the family of Israel should despise the covenant of their God, was more than pious Jews could bear. Against all these classes—lukewarm or faithless Jews, who cared only for their own profit, and scrupled not to cheat and impoverish their brethren, irritated and malicious neighbours, heartless and tyrannical rulers,—the psalmists hurled the most violent epithets,—"wicked," "impious," "doers of evil," "men of blood," "speakers of lies," "proud," "braggarts," "robbers," "scorners," "enemies to Jehovah," "rebels," "causeless enemies," "those that return evil for good." From a religious and moral point of view they could see no difference between them. Neither faithless Jew nor tyrannical heathen ruler believes in the divine government of the world. He forgets God, does not invoke Him, does not fear Him (Ps. ix., 18; xiv., 4; xxxvi., 2; l., 22); he thinks, though he does not say, "There is no God" (Ps. xiv., 1; *cf.* x., 4, xxxvi., 1). He can use the most cutting words to those who cannot venture to retaliate, for "who hears?" (Ps. lix., 7). He can commit the greatest outrages, for "Jehovah does not see" (Ps. x., 11, xciv., 7). He may indeed (if nominally a Jew) use the conventional religious forms, "bowing his head like a bulrush" (Isa. lviii., 5) at the public litanies. But he does so in order to circumvent God—so incredibly mean, as the psalmist thinks, is his conception of God. He has, in fact, adapted his religious views to his practical requirements; he thinks that God is even such an one as himself (Ps. l., 21); he has a delusive oracle in his heart which tells him just what he wishes to hear. This false god is the sin within him, which has taken the place of that divine instructor who dwells in each member of the faithful community. Listen to the psalmist:

"[That God is not, is] the divine oracle of Sin—
  To the wicked man within his heart;
  No dread of God is before his eyes.
  For he flatters Jehovah in subtlety—
  Jehovah will not discover the wickedness of his tongue.
  The words of his mouth are mischief and guile;
  He has left off acting wisely and well."
                              (Ps. xxxvi., 1–3.)

Strangely enough, a similar portrait is given of the righteous Job by the aged and narrow-minded Eliphaz:

> "Yea, thou destroyest religion,
> And dost dismiss devout meditation.
> For thine iniquity teaches thy mouth,
> And thou choosest the tongue of the subtle."*
>
> (Job xv., 4, 5.)

The only difference is that Job, according to Eliphaz, superadds to his wicked deeds a theoretical justification of his impiety, whereas the wicked men of the Psalms are not represented as at all intellectual. It is only in the First Psalm—the Psalm of the Two Ways—that we hear of a class of men called "scoffers," and this shows us that we must not look to the Psalms for a complete picture of Jewish society.

But what are the outrages of which the party of the wicked men has been guilty? They consist partly in the use of offensive expressions towards Israel and Israel's God, alternating with hypocritical professions of friendship, partly in slanderous misrepresentations of the righteous, addressed perhaps to the judge or to the Persian or Greek governor, partly in gross unfairness to the poor righteous in business transactions, partly in acts of physical

---
* *Cf.* Lecture IV.

violence. I will quote some passages from the Psalms which bear out this statement.

First, as to the speeches of the wicked men. As evidence I will quote two very sad passages. The tone is that of many a persecuted Jew in the long middle age:

> "Pity us, Jehovah, oh, pity us!
> For too long have we been sated with contempt;
> Yea, too long has our soul been sated
> With the mockery of the careless,
> The contempt of the proud."
> (Ps. cxxiii., 3, 4.)

And now for the companion passage:

> "Insult has broken my heart;
> Very grievous is the wound of my soul;
> I looked for a sympathiser, but there was none,
> And for comforters, but I found none.
> They gave me gall as my food,
> And in my thirst they gave me vinegar to drink."
> (Ps. lxix., 20, 21.)

By the "gall" and the "vinegar" the poet means bitter, scornful words. The speaker is faithful Israel, who is insulted because he is the "Servant of Jehovah." Hence in the same psalm we read: "The insults of those who insulted thee fell upon me." It appears from the context that the mockery of the enemies was called forth partly by the miserable condition of the faithful community, which seemed at its last gasp, chiefly by the forms and ceremonies of the Jewish religion. It is true the only form expressly mentioned is fasting.* This appears to be singled out here because it struck the observation of a bystander more than church litanies; it was in fact the climax of the attempts of the faithful to work upon their God. Elsewhere, however, we learn that the prayers of believers did not escape ridicule. So futile did these prayers appear, that the enemies could plausibly ask, "Where is thy God?" (Ps. xlii., 3, 4), and the wicked man could even venture to "curse at the attainment of his desire," and the "robber" to "contemn Jehovah" (Ps. x., 3). The favourite phrases of believers seem also to have been ridiculed; at least there is one most touching passage which gives an imaginary speech of the persecutors, and seems to imply this. One word or two in my reading of it is open to dispute, viz., in the third line, where I find a reference to the favourite title of God in the Second Isaiah's Prophecy of Restoration. But the received text cannot, in my opinion, be defended.

"All that see me laugh me to scorn ;
They open wide the lips ; they shake the head.

* So far as we can see, the forms most valued by the pious Jews of this period were the singing of praise, the recital of prayers, and fasting. Sabbath and Circumcision are nowhere mentioned in the Psalms.

(Forsooth,) his redeemer is Jehovah; (then) let Jehovah rescue him!
Let Jehovah deliver him, seeing He has such delight in him!"
(Ps. xxii., 7, 8.)

Sometimes, however, the persecuted righteous stand at bay, and meet their enemies with the poor man's weapon of prayer, an effectual, fervent prayer, which is confident of an answer.

> "Stilled be those lying lips
> Which speak against the righteous
> Proud words in haughtiness and scorn."
> (Ps. xxxi., 18.)

The scorn of the wicked rich for the righteous poor shows itself in one rather singular way. It seems as if the wicked preferred to use mean and disgraceful methods whenever they could. They sought to lull the righteous into a false security by professing to be their friends. Treachery plays a large part in the story of the Maccabees, and there is only too much reason to believe that the dread of it always lay in the background of the Jewish mind. One psalmist says:

> "There is nothing trustworthy in their speech,
> Their inward aim is ruin;
> An open grave is their throat,
> Though flattery glides from their tongue."
> (Ps. v., 9.)

Another characterises the wicked man thus:

> "His face is smoother than butter,
> But war is in his heart;
> His words are softer than oil,
> And yet are they javelins."
> (Ps. lv., 21.)

Next, as to the slander which forms another article in the indictment of the wicked. These are pious Israel's ejaculations:

> "Give me not over to the greed of my foes!
> For against me false witnesses have risen up,
> And they puff out (words of) injustice."
> (Ps. xxvii., 12.)

And again:

> "Witnesses who serve injustice arise,
> And with tricks they despoil me."
> (Ps. xxxv., 11.)

Here we have a reference to a common practice of avaricious and powerful men—to accuse innocent persons of some crime, such as theft, with the view of obtaining double restitution. The judges would of course share the plunder (*cf.* Mic. iii., 3). Or the accusation might be that of treason. How plausible such a charge might be in the dark years at the close of the Persian rule, and even at a later time, need not be said. Well might the church-nation pray,

"Deliver my soul, Jehovah, from the lying lip, from the deceitful tongue" (Ps. cxx., 2),—and then, in the words of the fine psalm at the end of the Book of Ecclesiasticus, give thanks to her Lord and King for deliverance "from the lips that forge lies," because "by an accusation to the king from an unrighteous tongue her soul had drawn nigh unto death" (Ecclus. li., 2-6).

Under these circumstances normal business relations between the two parties were impossible. Even if the psalmists exaggerate when they deny their opponents the least vestige of honesty (Ps. xii., 1), yet this very exaggeration bears witness to a social injustice which is inconsistent with commerce.* The petty details of commercial unfairness are of course not given. But we *are* told that "extortion and deceit depart not from the market-place" (Ps. lv., 11). No doubt this extortion was largely connected with money-lending. To lend money gratuitously to faithful Jews was meritorious (Ps. xxxvii., 26; cxii., 5), while to require usury was as bad as taking a bribe against the innocent (Ps. xv., 5).

That acts of personal violence were also committed by the Jewish oppressors, is not quite so easy to prove.

* Even in Ben Sira's time the relation of a rich man to a poor man was like that of a wolf to a lamb (Ecclus. xiii., 17-19).

The wicked of Jewish and those of heathen origin are not always easy to distinguish. Probably native officials were employed under the foreign governors, who misused their power, and became even more hated than the foreigners. In Proverbs xxviii., 3 (*cf.* v., 15) we read that "a wicked grandee [or tyrant] who oppresses the mean folk is like a sweeping rain which leaves no food," and in Psalm lii., 1, a psalmist thus apostrophises an unnamed offender:

" Why gloriest thou in mischief, thou grandee !
[And showest insolence] to the pious unceasingly ? "

In both cases the most natural interpretation is that a native tyrant is meant. Still more certain is the reference in the next passage that I shall quote. It shows that there were immoral men, Jews in name but not in soul, who did not scruple to shed blood when their wishes could only so be gratified. The more pious section of the Jewish people prays to God thus:

" Take not away my soul with sinners,
 Nor my life with men of blood,
 On whose hands are (the marks of) crimes,
 And their right hands are full of bribes."
                                    (Ps. xxvi., 9, 10.)

These men, as it appears, belonged to an association. They had common principles and interests, and therefore formed a party. So that, when pious Israel personified says, in the same psalm (ver. 5),

"I hate the congregation of evil doers,
And will not sit in the conclave of the wicked,"

he means that he recognises the utter inconsistency of his own principles with those of the opposite party. He hates them, he says elsewhere (Ps. cxxxix., 21), because they hate and oppose Jehovah, and it is the hardest problem that he knows to reconcile their continued existence with the divine justice.

You will see that I am of opinion that the Psalter is a historical document of a high order—that I am in no doubt either as to its date, or as to the credibility of its expressed or implied statements, with the qualifications which I have mentioned. I hold the post-exilic date of every part of the Psalms to have been abundantly proved, and the credibility of their statements seems to me to be confirmed by the historical and prophetical records already referred to. That there was a strong tension of feeling among pious Jews is plain, and this quite accounts for the vehement language of the psalmists, who were truthful men, even if naturally prone, like the prophets before them, to some exaggeration.

It would, however, be unsafe to assume that the division of the Jews into the wicked rich and the righteous poor, which pervades so much of the later literature, is an exhaustive classification. The righteous poor are collectively the self-sacrificing Servant of Jehovah described in Isaiah liii. They are the inner circle, the few really fine grapes on the cluster. Side by side with them—observers of the law like themselves, only not so strict; frequenters of the temple, only not so constant—are the great majority of those who call upon the name of Jehovah. They are not perfect in humility or in obedience, and are liable to be carried away by the evil example of the wicked. They need the guidance and instruction of those who are firmer in faith, and it is to them that the expounders of the law, the writers of prophecies, and those wise moral teachers, some of whom have composed psalms and others pointed sayings and eloquent discourses, devote their ceaseless energies. It is for their use that the noble prayer was written:

" Search me out, O God, and know my heart,
  Try me, and know my thoughts,
  And see if there be any practice of covetousness in me,
  And lead me in the ancient road " * ;

and it was of the teachers of righteousness (whom I shall next describe) that the author of Daniel prophesied that "the teachers should shine like the splendour of the firmament, and they that turn the many to righteousness like the stars for ever and ever" (Dan. xii., 3).

* Ps. cxxxix., 24 ; the speaker in vv. 19–24 is personified Israel.

LECTURE IV.

Jewish Wisdom; its Meaning, Object, and Varieties.

IN the remaining portion of this historical sketch I shall endeavour to complete the proof of the rich variety of life in early Judaism. And I shall first of all ask you to study with me the great educational movement of the period, out of which proceeded the singular phenomenon called Jewish Wisdom. Its origin is a matter of conjecture. Most probably, however, it originated in the consciousness that, if not only individuals but whole classes of society were to become righteous (and this was known to be the condition of the divine favour), there was a need of some new and attractive presentation of moral and religious truth. The ideal of many of the noblest minds was that expressed in the opening of the First Psalm:

" Happy is the man who delights in the fear * of Jehovah,
And meditates on His law day and night " (Ps. i., 2).

* Adopting a probable correction.

But it must soon have become evident that there was a large number to whom this description would never apply, because of the many difficulties in the volume of Scripture, at which they were sure to stumble.* Hence the idea appears to have arisen, that if that volume were studied by wise men who were in touch with the people, it might be possible to make an abstract of such religious truths as even men of the world (if the phrase may be used) could recognise and live by. If this view be sound, we may naturally expect that many patriotic teachers would be deep students of Scripture and earnest observers of the established forms. They would, in short, be fervently religious men, though they might not always think it expedient to display their fervour before their disciples. There would, however, also be a minority who would not be satisfied with elementary instruction, but would seek to carry on the intellectual movement of the past. Some of them would exhibit in their teaching a perfect fusion of morality and religion; they would produce works to which after-ages would look up as, not, indeed, in the received sense, revelation, but as not less precious, not less truly divine, than the Law or the prophecies. And there would be others of a sceptical turn, whose

* "He that devotes himself to the Law is filled therewith, but the profane person stumbles thereat" (Ecclus. xxxii., 15).

writings would only escape oblivion by some happy chance.

Thus we may expect to find, and we actually do find, three varieties of didactic and reflective ethical literature—two representing a more or less complete fusion of the ethical and the orthodox religious spirit, and one expressing a distinctly heterodox or sceptical tendency. We find, too, that this reflective literature claimed a high antiquity. Just as sacred lyric poetry attached itself to the glorious name of David, so the new moral literature claimed as its originator the idealised Solomon.* A post-exilic writer has been at the pains to show in what various forms King Solomon's wisdom expressed itself. Solomon was of course a just and skilful ruler—that more than one older writer had brought out very clearly. But he was also a much wider-minded man than most rulers. Listen to the beautiful little narrative in which this idea is conveyed :

"And God gave Solomon wisdom and insight and a resourceful mind.† Solomon's wisdom was greater than that of all the men of the east and than all the wisdom of Egypt. He was wiser than all men, wiser than Ethan the Ezrahite, and Heman and Calcol and Darda, the sons of Mahol ; and his fame reached all the nations

---

* There may of course have been a pre-exilic Wisdom-Literature, but how (if such existed) it stood related to the literature of the post-exilic Jewish sages, it is impossible to say.

† A mind "seething" with new ideas (corrected text).

round about. And he spoke three thousand proverbs, and his songs were a thousand and five. And he spoke of trees, from the cedar in Lebanon to the hyssop which springs out of the wall; he spoke also of beasts and birds and reptiles and fishes. And men came from all countries to hear the wisdom of Solomon, from all the kings of the earth who had heard of his wisdom" (1 Kings iv., 29–34).

No explanation of this is as reasonable as that which finds in it a reference to our Book of Proverbs,* to our Song of Songs, and to our Book of Job. It is true that we have only one "song," the title of which claims Solomonic authorship, but this title may without violence be so rendered as to make Solomon the author of an indefinite number of songs. About twenty plants and thirteen animals are mentioned in that fascinating poem, the Canticles, and it may easily have been supposed that in Solomon's other songs many more plants and animals were referred to. Beasts and birds are also described with great fulness in the Book of Job, and the writer of the eulogium on Solomon probably means to imply that Solomon outdid the author of even that poetic masterpiece.

But was there no conception of wisdom, no attempt at the moral instruction of the young, in pre-exilic times? Certainly. Some time in the seventh cen-

* See Ecclus. xlvii., 17, where the Hebrew text shows that the writer is thinking of Prov. i., 6. He evidently supposes Solomon's proverbs to be exactly analogous to those in our Book of Proverbs.

tury an insertion was made in Genesis xviii., to show that the blessings promised to Abraham were conditional on his instilling right religion and morality into his children and household (vv. 17-19). And whatever be the exact date of the exhortations in Deuteronomy (*e.g.*, iv., 10; vi., 7, 20 *ff.*; xi., 19) to instruct children in the sacred history and law, we may presume that they are in the spirit of the framers of the earlier Deuteronomic law-book. This new didactic movement was an indirect result of the preaching of Isaiah, who succeeded in bringing home to the best minds of the next age the fact of the general moral deficiency. It was Isaiah too who, first among the canonical writers, expressed the intuition of Jehovah's wisdom (Isa. xxxi., 2). It is true that some belief in the divine wisdom may have existed before his time through Babylonian influence on the Canaanites.* Still it is most improbable that this belief was as pure and, religiously, as vital as the intuition of Isaiah. With what loving reverence does this prophet speak of the "plan" of the world's great Governor, and how stern is his contempt for the futile schemes of those who do not "ask at Jehovah's mouth" (Isa. xxx., 2)! For his own part he does not care to be called a "wise man." Wisdom in a religious sense is still too much identified with skill

---

* The god Ea was called "lord of wisdom and understanding."

Jewish Wisdom

in the performance of traditional rites or in the recitation of magic formulæ. It is better to be Jehovah's mouthpiece, and to ascribe to Him all the honour of that marvellous insight which has made Isaiah the wisest of the Israelites of his time.

Let us now briefly sketch the outlines of the early popular idea of wisdom. Great rulers, like David and Solomon, were said to have "the wisdom of God," or of "God's angel" (2 Sam. xiv., 17, 20; 1 Kings iii., 28), because they could give rapid and just judicial decisions. Politicians, too, could be likened to incarnate divine oracles; Ahithophel is an instance of this (2 Sam. xvi., 23). Soothsayers, priests, and prophets were revered as wise, because they claimed to tell men the will of God, though Jeremiah calls the pen of the scribes who wrote down the supposed wisdom of the law-books a "lying pen" (Jer. viii., 8), because their work threatened to check his own more spiritual preaching. Poets, too, to the Israelites as well as to the Arabs, must have appeared to have more than earthly wisdom; they partook of the inspiration of the prophet.*
And framers of apologues or parables like those of Jotham and the "wise woman" † of Tekoa were

---

* Note that Balaam the seer is said to "take up a parable," or rather to "utter a poem" (*mashal*) in Num. xxiii., xxiv.

† Judg. ix., 8-15 ; 2 Sam. xiv., 2. The phrase "wise woman" is used in a different sense in Jer. ix., 17.

doubtless looked up to as in their degree divinely gifted; indeed, even the traditional skill of craftsmen was devoutly traced to a divine gift, as the Hebrew legends of the origin of culture prove. On the other hand, it ought to be mentioned that there was also a current story in which even the knowledge of good and evil was represented as an illegitimate acquisition. It was a first attempt to account for the mingled grandeur and poverty of human life. Man was like the divine beings in knowledge, but sadly unlike them in his liability to sickness and death. It was reserved for a later age to arrive at the conviction that true wisdom was a tree of life.

Whether any fruitful contact between the incipient wisdom of the Israelites and that of their neighbours took place in pre-exilic times, we know not. Jeremiah speaks of the wisdom of Teman (Jer. xlix., 7), and it is just conceivable that the story of Job, partly moralised, may have come from Edom shortly before the Exile. At any rate, such contact existed (as we shall see) in post-exilic times. The story of Solomon's wisdom itself suggests this. No stress need be laid on the particular peoples mentioned by the narrator. The point to dwell upon is that the reputed wisdom of Solomon was cosmopolitan. There were wise men among other nations, just as there were true though unconscious worshippers of Jehovah (Mal. i., 11). Solomon was superior to them, because, as the Jews believed, he knew the one true God better than they did, and they came to him for stimulus and instruction. From the Prologue to Proverbs we see that this entirely corresponds to the temper of some of the Jewish sages. One of these makes personified Wisdom exclaim (Prov. viii., 4):

> "Unto you, O men, I call,
> And my appeal is to the human race";

and later on, in the grandest of her soliloquies, she declares that of all God's created works she delighted most in the race of man (Prov. viii., 31).

It is true, no attempt is made in the two earlier Books of Wisdom to make practical use of the principle involved in these passages. But the universal relation of Wisdom is asserted, and it only required time for the Jewish sages to awaken to the consciousness of the necessary practical inferences. The author of the so-called Wisdom of Solomon is the bravest and boldest of them all, for he is willing to take as well as give instruction, and, like Philo, fervently believes in the reality of ethnic inspiration. But at present we must be satisfied with the larger outlook already obtained by post-exilic sages. This was not lost even by the author of Ecclesiasticus, though he lays more stress on forms of religion than did the earlier wise men. To complete his education, he says, the wise man must "travel through the land of strange nations," must "try good things and evil among men," and "if the great Lord will," and he is "filled with the spirit of understanding," the "nations" in general, as well as the congregation, will "declare his praise" (Ecclus. xxxix., 4, 10). For not with Jews, as Jews, but with men did Wisdom "lay an eternal foundation, and with their offspring shall she be had in trust" (Ecclus. i., 15). In fact, all the wise men have grasped the grand idea of a human family. It may also be found in the Psalter. But that important Book has in this respect one very sad limitation. The sufferings of the Jews, and especially of the *élite* among them, were so great towards the close of the Persian empire that, by a pathetic fallacy, it seemed as if all mankind except the Jews were morally worthless. Those psalms into which a sense of something like the brotherhood of nations begins to penetrate are for various reasons later than 332 B.C. I call this limitation of view a sad one. It is unfortunate that the great picture of the missionary Servant of Jehovah should have had, comparatively speaking, so little effect. Still a perfectly adequate cause has been adduced for this unprogressiveness: psychological miracles are not to be expected. Not till the coming of the great Macedonian reconciler of East and West could there be a presentiment of the truth of the divine education, not only of Israel, but of the human race.

One may be thankful that the Psalter does not entirely belong to the Persian period. Among the debts which we owe to the later psalmists, do not let us overlook these striking words:

" He that disciplines the nations, cannot He punish—
He that teaches mankind knowledge?" (Ps. xciv., 10.)

They imply just that notion which we find in the story of Solomon's wisdom, viz., that wisdom, divinely given wisdom, is accessible to all men; but they add that the object of the divine instructor is not merely theoretical but practical. A moralist of a later date puts this in a more attractive form:

" The mercy of a man is upon his neighbour,
But the mercy of the Lord is upon all flesh;
Reproving, disciplining, and teaching,
And bringing back, as a shepherd does his flock."
(Ecclus. xviii., 13.)

A fine saying, is it not? and it suggests one of the chief requisites of an educator,—a friendly feeling towards his pupils. God's patient, considerate instruction is the result of His mercy or loving-kindness, and He desires a similar loving-kindness among fellow-citizens, that they may be educationally useful to each other. In default of this loving-kindness, a man deserves no better title than "fool," for

"To commit a crime is sport to a fool."
(Prov. x., 23.)

The Jewish teachers were in general very hopeless of making anything of such persons. Once we find the noble sentiment that

"Even a senseless man may be taught,
And a wild ass's colt may be caught."*
(Job. xi., 12.)

But more often we find nothing but prophecies of evil for the "fool," and a recommendation not to spare stripes for his back. That a "fool" was ever reformed by this treatment, we do not hear. A proverb assures us that

"Even if thou pound a fool in the midst of his fellows,†
Thou wilt not remove his foolishness from him"
(Prov. xxvii., 22);

and another that

"A rebuke penetrates into one that has understanding;
(But) a fool, when he is smitten, makes light of it."
(Prov. xvii., 10.)

---

* The rhyme corresponds to the assonance in the original, according to a very possible correction of the corrupt Hebrew text ("The Book of Job," *Expositor*, June, 1897).
† Compare the Septuagint.

With this exception, however, the wise men themselves admit no limit to their influence. It is useless to assert *a priori* that wise maxims can have done little to keep the Jewish youth in the right paths. Experience taught the ancients otherwise in many different countries. To us these Hebrew proverbs may seem at first sight to be destitute of motive power, but a close inspection will modify this opinion. Provisionally, the Hebrew Wisdom was of the greatest practical service. It passed necessarily into something widely different, but not without leaving a permanent impression on the form of the teaching which succeeded it. How indeed could it have been otherwise? for the best men of the time were among these proverbial teachers, and in reading the finest parts of Proverbs even we can appreciate the force of the saying that

"The fruit of the righteous is a tree of life,
And the wise man is a winner of souls."
(Prov. xi., 30.)

How carefully the so-called Wisdom was planned, we see from the strong secular element in it. If the fear of Jehovah is the first part of the instruction which it gives, the art of getting on in the world is the second. It is almost amusing to notice that the same writer who says that wisdom is far better than riches also informs us that wisdom is the best road to wealth (Prov. iii., 14–16; viii., 18–19). In fact, one of the most characteristic terms for wisdom means ability to steer well, and the general spirit of the sayings of the wise men can scarcely be called idealistic. The tone which pervades them is that of a calm reasonableness; indeed, we are told in so many words that "he that is of a cool spirit is a man of understanding" (Prov. xvii., 27). Now and then this "coolness" even seems to a modern to degenerate into meanness:

" A clever man sees a misfortune coming, and hides himself,
While those who are simple pass on and suffer for it."
(Prov. xxii., 3.)

This, however, is merely a relic of that old nomadic love of craft or subtlety,* from which even David was not exempt.

On the whole, the wise men recommended energetic action, such as befits those who are conscious of rectitude and of enjoying the divine favour.

But what of the religious aspect of this proverbial wisdom? We may easily be led to underrate this. It ought, however, to be emphatically stated that the

* Even the strongly religious author of the Prologue to Proverbs three times makes "subtlety" or "cleverness" an essential part of wisdom (i., 4; viii., 5, 12). On the other hand, "subtlety" and "subtle" are used with a bad connotation in Job (v., 12–13; xv., 5). *Cf.* Lecture III.

wise men presuppose more than they expressly state. Their teaching may at first sight seem almost purely secular, but it takes for granted the theory of earthly retribution, which is a fundamental doctrine of the Law, and it lays stress on precisely those moral qualities which follow from the due performance of the commandments. In recommending wisdom, those early moralists certainly meant to recommend the Law, or at least to show that orthodox religion was not merely not inconsistent with, but even conducive to, worldly success. To call their wisdom either secular or, in a modern sense, utilitarian would be a mistake. Its religious character indeed is not unfrequently affirmed. Thus we hear that

"The fear of Jehovah is a discipline for wisdom,
And before honour is humility"
(Prov. xv., 33);

i. e., the constant practice of religion is the right school of wisdom, and humility (which, as the later writers teach, is one half of righteousness) will be finally rewarded with honour.

"The fear of Jehovah prolongs days,
But the years of the wicked will be shortened"
(Prov. x., 27);
"The way [*i. e.*, procedure] of Jehovah is a stronghold to the innocent,
But ruin to the workers of iniquity"
(x., 29);

"He that walks in his uprightness fears Jehovah,
But he that is perverse in his ways despises Him"
(Prov. xiv., 2);

i. e., religion and morality are identical.

"He that oppresses the poor despises the poor man's Maker,
But Jehovah honours him that has pity on the needy"
(xiv., 31);

i. e., morality is based on the common relation of all men to the Creator.

"Shĕól and Abaddon [*i. e.*, all parts of the nether world] are before Jehovah;
How much more then the hearts of mankind!
The eyes of Jehovah are in every place,
Observing the evil and the good"
(xv., 3, 11);

two beautiful expressions for the omniscience of Jehovah—a divine attribute which became more fully realised after the time of Jeremiah. For we cannot doubt that the observation spoken of extends to the heart and conscience. A psalmist of the Greek period finely says:

"Out of heaven Jehovah looked down,
He beheld all the race of men;
From his sure habitation He gazed
Upon all who dwell on the earth—
He who formed the hearts of them all,
Who takes note of all their works."
(Ps. xxxiii., 13-15.)

Another wise man says that

"The sacrifice of the wicked is an abomination to Jehovah,
But the prayer of the upright is His delight"
(Prov. xv., 8),

implying, by the way, that prayer is the best part of the sacrificial service, and is acceptable even without sacrifice. And another goes even farther, and says:

"To do the just and right thing
Is pre-eminent with Jehovah above sacrifice."
(xxi., 3; *cf.* ver. 27.)

I will now quote one of the finest religious sayings in Proverbs:

"Disclose what thou wouldest do to Jehovah,
And thy purposes shall be established."
(xvi., 3.)

Of course this only refers to righteous purposes. The wise man cannot mean that we can make God our fellow-conspirator against our enemies. On the contrary, as another proverb says:

"Rejoice not, when thine enemy falls,*
And let not thine heart be glad when he is overthrown;
Lest Jehovah see it, and it displease Him,
And he turn away His wrath from thine enemy."
(xxiv., 17.)

* *I. e.*, when a calamity overtakes him.

The idea is that a malicious joy at the misfortunes of another is displeasing to God, even if that other be an enemy of the righteous, and that if, knowing God's will but doing it not, the righteous man commits this sin, he will be more deserving of punishment than his adversary.

And again:

> "If thine enemy hunger, give him food;
> Or if he thirst, give him water to drink!
> For hot coals thou takest away,*
> And Jehovah will recompense thee."
>
> (Prov. xxv., 21, 22.)

The meaning is, that the new relation created by this unexpected hospitality will supersede the old pernicious relation of oppressor and oppressed. The "hot coals" of strife (see xxvi., 21) will have been firmly grasped and removed, and the recompense due to those who relieve the needy will be paid by Jehovah. Here there is a chance for the righteous to melt the hard hearts of the wicked, and save them from the otherwise certain retribution. Or if this be too high a flight for most minds, yet all can understand that

> "If a man's ways please Jehovah,
> He reconciles even his enemies to him."
>
> (xvi., 7.)

* Adopting a correction of the text, which relieves the proverb-writer from the charge of ethical inconsistency.

Evidently the Jewish world has made some progress since personified Israel prayed:

" Put to shame and dishonour be those that seek my soul,
Turned back and abashed be those that plan my hurt ;
Be they as chaff before the wind,
And Jehovah's angel pursuing them ;
Be their way dark and slippery,
And Jehovah's angel thrusting them."
(Ps. xxxv., 4-6.)

We must remember, however, that it is not in general of individuals but of hostile communities or factions that the psalmists speak. Individuals can more easily be reached by kindness than bodies of men. Also that the same collection of Jewish proverbs contains this startling saying:

" Jehovah has made everything for its special end ;
Yea, even the wicked for the day of trouble."
(Prov. xvi., 4.)

This reminds us of a psalmist who, looking back on the oppressive rule and sudden collapse of the Persian empire, attributes it to a deep design of Jehovah which a "fool" cannot understand:

" When the wicked spring as the herbage,
And all the workers of iniquity blossom,
It is (only) that they may be destroyed forever,
Whilst Thou, Jehovah, art King eternally."
(Ps. xcii., 7, 8.)

Both psalmist and wise man assume that there are human beings who are irredeemably bad, viz., those Jews who have turned aside from truth to serve a lie, and those heathen who have banded themselves together to put out the one great light which God has set in a dark world—the light of the covenant people of Israel. Such wicked men cannot repent; they must be wiped out of existence. Their "disproportioned sin"

> " Jars against nature's chime, and with harsh din
> Breaks the fair music that all creatures make
> To their great Lord." *

But both psalmist and wise man have learned to be more patient than formerly seemed possible. The "day of Jehovah" must be waited for. It is useless to cry out, " Rouse Thee; why sleepest Thou, Jehovah?" (Ps. xliv., 24.) For the present, the Omniscient One tolerates bad as well as good; He lets both grow together till the harvest. As a wise man says:

> " The poor man and the exactor jostle each other;
> Jehovah lightens the eyes of both."
> (Prov. xxix., 13.)

It is in fact this coexistence of good and bad, wise and foolish, within the same community which makes

* Milton, " At a Solemn Musick."

a strong central authority indispensable. Could the individualising method of the teachers called wise men be universally applied, it would still be difficult to repress the anarchic tendencies of the multitude. For

> "Without a curb* people become unruly;
> But he that keeps the law, happy is he."
> (Prov. xxix., 18.)

The term "the law" means here that condensed extract and practical application of the teaching of the Scriptures which was prepared by the wise men for their pupils. The misfortune was that the central authority was in the hands of heathen rulers, who had not the same moral standards as the wise men. Hence the tone of the proverbs respecting the king is somewhat surprising. Was the king in some passages a native ruler? Was he even sometimes the Messiah? These are the passages in question:

(i.) "The king's favour is for an intelligent servant,
But a base one experiences his wrath."
(xiv., 35.)

(ii.) "Jehovah' oracle is on the lips of the king;
His mouth will not offend against justice."
(xvi., 10.)

---

*Here the importance of a corrected text is specially apparent. The received text has "Without vision," which is supposed to mean "without prophetic revelation."

(iii.) "Loving-kindness and truth guard the king;
 And by loving-kindness he supports his throne."
          (Prov. xx., 28.)

(iv.) "Take away the dross from the silver,
 And the whole of it comes out refined;
 Take away the wicked from before the king,
 And by righteousness his throne is established."
          (xxv., 4, 5.)

(v.) "My son, fear Jehovah and the king,
 And meddle not with those who hate them;
 For suddenly their calamity will rise,
 And the ruin of the haters will come unawares"
          (xxiv., 21, 22.)

(vi.) "Three things are of stately walk,
 Yea, four of stately going:
 The lion—the hero among the beasts,
 That nothing makes to turn back,
 The cock* that (proudly) lifts itself up, and the he-goat,
 And a king, the champion of his people."
          (xxx., 29–31.)

There is also a curious group of counsels (xxxi., 1–9) described as "Words of a king; a proverb [or, poem] with which his mother instructed him." The sayings, however, are plainly artificial and of very late origin; they need not detain us now.

The sayings in the former group are much more interesting. But not even all these have a clear note

---

* If this rendering is correct it favours, and indeed requires, a very late date for the passage. See "Cock" in *Encyclopædia Biblica*.

of reality. A non-Jewish king might conceivably be idealised in a more or less complimentary lyric poem, but hardly in proverbs designed for the popular instruction. Surely it is only the last two of the first group which refer to contemporary kings—the first to a Græco-Egyptian, the second probably to a Maccabæan prince. The four preceding ones, however, are specially interesting to students of religion. They represent a Messianic element in the Book of Proverbs like that represented by most of the royal hymns in the Psalter. The writers look forward with much assurance to the speedy renewal of the native royalty, and seek to instil into the minds of their young disciples lofty ideas of the kingly character. The sayings remind us of Psalms xlv. and lxxii. No such Messianic element exists in the Book of Ecclesiasticus, though that interesting book does contain a prayer of considerable beauty for the deliverance and glorification of Israel. (Ecclus. xxxvi., 1–17).

There is no trace, however, that the wise men had any systematised Messianic belief; they seem completely to neglect the incipient theories of the later prophetic writers. It is not an emperor of the world, but a blameless, modest-minded king of Israel whom they set before us, though, in accordance apparently with a fixed rule, they do not once mention the name of Israel. For this king they patiently wait, because they trust Jehovah not to leave them always under the rule of the Ptolemies, however endurable this might be, compared with the rule of the last Persian kings. They are content that the final doomsday should be put off for a season, because they observe that even now the righteous are not altogether forsaken, and that individuals at any rate receive an adequate earthly recompense for their righteousness. Probably, too, the majority of the wise men were limited in the expression of their views by educational considerations. "To fear Jehovah and to shun evil" was all that the ordinary man required.

For some of the wise men, however, this severely practical view of wisdom was not enough. There is one passage even in the Book of Proverbs which suggests an interest in cosmic phenomena, and there are other passages in Job. It is true, the former passage occurs in the Prologue of Proverbs, which has a unity of its own, and is very distinct in many respects from the body of the work. Here is the description. It consists of five stanzas of four lines each *:

"Jehovah produced me as the firstfruits of His creation,
   The earliest of His primæval works;

* On the text, see article "On Some Obscure Passages" etc., *Jewish Quarterly Review*, Oct., 1897.

For from of old was I woven together,
From the beginning, from the first days of the world.

"When the floods were not, I was brought forth,
When there were no fountains abounding with water,
Before the mountains were deeply fixed,
Before the hills was I brought forth.*

"Ere He had made the land and the grass,
And had clothed with green the clods of mother-earth;
When He prepared the heavens, I was there,
When He marked out a circle over the ocean;

"When He established the clouds above,
When He made firm the founts of the ocean,
When He appointed to the sea its bound,
That the waters should not transgress His command;

"Then was I daily beside Him as an artificer,
Sporting continually before Him,
Sporting in the elaboration † of his earth,
And having my delight in the race of man."
                                    (Prov. viii., 22–31.)

This is certainly one of the greatest passages in the Wisdom-literature. It states that pre-existent Wisdom was the artificer of the world, one in purpose and in act with the creative Deity, and, taken with the context, it implies that Wisdom introduces her disciples to the study of cosmic phenomena as well

---

* This resembles the description of the first man, who is primæval wisdom personified, in Job xv., 7, 8.

† This appears to be a certain correction of the text. It probably decides the correctness of the rendering "artificer" in line 1 of the stanza.

as of practical ethics. The beginning or first part of wisdom is, according to the writer, the fear of Jehovah; or, to widen our definition without misrepresenting his meaning, it is a combination of religion with a certain practical cleverness. But the latter part is something of a more refined, esoteric type. It is the contemplation of God's works in nature, and it is just such a contemplation of the ideals of which those works are the expression, or, in Hebrew phraseology, of pre-existent Wisdom, which God Himself did not disdain when He made the world. For, as another Hebrew poet, one of the writers of the Book of Job, finely says:

> "When He made a weight for the wind,
> And determined the waters by measure,
> Then He beheld and studied her well,
> He set her up and fathomed her depths."
> (Job xxviii., 26, 27.)

In fact, the Book of Job contains more than one passage in which the larger conception of human wisdom is clearly expressed. For instance, the author of the Speeches of Jehovah certainly encourages the observation of nature. He has not, indeed, the modern, scientific spirit, and looks at nature in a poetic, imaginative way, with an underlying didactic object. But we must not underrate the importance of this. To be interested in nature is the first step to seeking to comprehend her. Gladly would I quote some of this writer's fine pictures of animal life, but I have only space for a series of naïve questions to which there are somewhat striking parallels in the sacred Zoroastrian literature. Hebrew affinities are not wanting, however. The first couplet, which speaks of a visit to the divine stores of snow and hail, reminds us of the story of Enoch as developed in the book which bears Enoch's name.*

" Hast thou (ever) come to the store-chambers of the snow,
And seen the store-keepers of the hail,—
Which I have reserved for the time of trouble,
For the day of battle and war?

" By what way does the mist part
That it may sprinkle cool moisture on the earth?
Who cleft a conduit for the rain-torrent,
And a way for the flashes of the storm,—

" To send rain on a land without men,
On the wilderness wherein are no people,
To satisfy the utter desolation,
And to cause the thirsty land to put forth fresh herbage?

" Out of whose womb came the ice?
And the hoar-frost of heaven—who begot it?

* Enoch lx., 17 ; *cf.* lxix., 23.

> The waters close together as if a stone,
> And the surface of the deep hides itself.

> "Dost thou bind the knots of the Pleiades?
> Or loose the fetters of Orion?
> Canst thou bring out the Hyades at its season?
> And guide the Bear and her offspring?*

> "Knowest thou the laws of heaven?
> Dost thou appoint its influence on the earth?
> Canst thou send up a command to the cloud
> That abundance of water may cover thee?" †

The irony of the questions is unmistakable. But their object is not merely to humble Job by giving him a sense of his limitations, but to encourage him to step out of himself into the great picture-gallery of the outer world. The poet, who is also a wise man, agrees neither with Job and his friends, as described in the dialogues, nor with an editor who, in opposition to the poet whose work he manipulates, asserts that the "only proper study of mankind" is practical religion. Let me read a part of the last strophe of the poem referred to:

> "Whence then proceeds wisdom?
> And where is the place of understanding?
> Seeing that it is hidden from the eyes of all living,
> And kept close from the birds of the sky.

---

* The renderings of the names of the constellations are not altogether certain.

† Job xxxviii., 22–27, 29–34 (from a corrected text). See *J. Q. R.*, Oct., 1897.

> "The abyss and the nether world say,
> The report of her has reached our ears.
> God has marked the way to her,
> He is acquainted with her place."*

Wisdom, then, is not independent of God, who, indeed, was the first to find her out. This discovery and its importance for the creative process are explained in the last quatrain, which I have already quoted.† And then, unexpectedly enough, comes the following only too orthodox statement:

> "And he said to man, Behold, the fear of Jehovah—that is wisdom, and to shun evil is understanding." ‡

I do not say that the author of this addition was a man of no ideas, but I say that he differed from the author of the poem, who certainly did not mean by his grand eulogy of the higher Wisdom to discourage men from interesting themselves in nature. This new writer had no poetic imagination, and, as might be expected, he writes in prose and not in verse.

It was remarked just now that the wise man who wrote the Speeches of Jehovah does not agree with all his colleagues. But on one point he and all the greatest of the wise men are agreed—there are no breaks in the consistency of the world. There is a place, we are told in Proverbs (xvi., 4), even for the

* Job xxviii., 20–23.   † See p. 150.   ‡ Job xxviii., 28.

wicked in God's scheme of things, and there must be a fundamental harmony between nature and morality. To thoughtful Jewish theists God revealed Himself as the All-wise. There never was a time when the divine Wisdom was not. There was never any combat (such as the dialogues in Job appear to presuppose) between Jehovah and the dragon of chaos*; on chaos the eulogist of Wisdom is eloquently silent. Nor can he admit the idea of an arbitrary omnipotence. "God," as Hooker, surnamed the Judicious, said, "is a law to Himself"; "His wisdom hath stinted the effects of His power." And so potent, so full of vitality, is this wise and beneficent law, that it is impossible to an Oriental thinker to regard it otherwise than as a person. And what a person! Work is to Him † a pastime; the elaboration of the world not a six-days' occupation but a continual and exquisite delight; the Creator needs no Sabbath rest, for He cannot be fatigued. Why, here is the saying so finely devised for the incarnate Logos in the spiritual Gospel, "My Father worketh hitherto, and I work." ‡ The universe is, as

---

* The descriptions of Behemoth and Leviathan (on which see *Expositor*, July, 1897, or *Encyclopædia Biblica*) form no part of the true Speeches of Jehovah. The author of the dialogues does, however, refer to the chaos-dragon, called Leviathan.

† It is, of course, accidental that "Wisdom" is personified as a woman (the Hebrew word for wisdom being feminine).

‡ John v., 17.

Jewish Wisdom

Emerson has expressed it, a "divine improvisation"; its architect is the "Eternal Child." Surely this is one of the very finest conceptions in the Old Testament. It stands there quite alone; but not less unique is more than one conception in the spiritual Gospel in the New Testament. The ideal thus expressed cannot safely be disregarded by those who would have a joyous as well as a deeply thoughtful religion.

And now we have to ask, What other forms of thought are most nearly related to this strange new conception of the divine Wisdom? The inquisitive spirit for which the varied scenes of human life are too narrow a field is the same which pervades the celestial physics of the Book of Enoch; it has found an imaginative (mythological) expression in the story of Enoch,* who was instructed by the angels in the secrets of the tripartite universe. Allusions to this story in its earlier form occur in Genesis v., 21-24, and again in a prophecy of Ezekiel (xxviii., 3), who says, addressing the Prince of Tyre:

"Forsooth, thou art wiser than Enoch; there is no secret that can be hidden from thee."

I ought to explain that this rendering presupposes a necessary and easy correction of the text. Anyone

* See article "Enoch" in Messrs. A. & C. Black's *Encyclopædia Biblica*.

can see that the expression "wiser than Daniel" is most improbable in this connection and in Ezekiel's period. On the other hand, this prophet must have known of Enoch as an explorer of secrets, and the tradition which had reached him was doubtless connected with some report of the natural philosophy of the Babylonians. It is true, the authors of the Book of Enoch far outrun Ezekiel, but so does the description of the divine Wisdom in parts of Proverbs and Job far surpass the meagre hints given by the Second Isaiah.*

But we must look farther afield for affinities to the personified divine Wisdom. Some scholars will, I know, object to this. They are of opinion that nearly all the strange new developments of the post-exilic period can be explained as native Jewish growths, and they think that this view harmonises best with the self-isolating tendency of the age of Ezra. This is, I think, a great mistake. The laws of the human mind fought against the self-isolating tendency which these scholars refer to. Oriental influences of all kinds made themselves felt, first of all by the people, and then by its religious guides. More especially in the Greek period, to which the Prologue of Proverbs certainly, or almost certainly, belongs, there was a fertilisation of the intellectual

* Isa. xl., 13, 14.

soil by new ideas throughout the Jewish world. Many Jews migrated to Egypt, especially to Alexandria, and we know that in ancient Egypt the personification of divine attributes was carried to a great extent.* It is a false assumption that ancient Egyptian ideas could not influence Greek and Jewish society in Alexandria. Persian influences, too, were still more strongly felt by the Jews after the conquests of Alexander. In the present state of the history of Zoroastrianism some reserve seems called for, but it is reasonable to hold that the stress laid in Zoroastrianism on wisdom as the chief divine attribute, and on the distinction between the heavenly wisdom † and that "acquired by the ear," had some effect on the Jews, though it would immediately affect only those Jews who lived in or near Persia. I am not so bold as to assume that the conception of the heavenly wisdom which was the earliest of Ahura-Mazda's creations was taken over directly and adapted by the author of the Prologue of Proverbs, and simply hold that the more advanced religious philosophy of Zoroastrianism stimulated the growth of a new Jewish religious philosophy, which centred in the belief in an all-wise and therefore not, strictly

* Wiedemann, *Gesch. Aeg.*, p. 53; *cf.* Brimmer, *Three Essays*, etc., p. 29.

† See *Zendavesta* by Darmesteter and Mills (Sacred Books of the East) and *cf.* Cheyne, *Expositor*, v. (1892), 78, 79.

speaking, all-powerful Being, the Creator and Governor of the world of nature and of man. To assume Platonic and Stoic influences seems to me both unnecessary and unsafe.

Here I might pause, but can I be expected to leave untouched the true Book of Job to which the two beautiful poems from which I have quoted form appendices? And how could I let the patriarch Enoch be separated from the patriarch Job—the one the representative of physical, the other of moral philosophy? The former came into his full inheritance long after the latter. Obviously the life of Enoch did not at first take much hold on thoughtful Jews. That after 365 years God could no longer spare such a pious and large-minded man, but took him into His immediate presence—this early departure of Enoch, in spite of its extraordinary circumstances, and however much it stimulated speculation, did not touch the heart. But the story of Job, who fell from the height of happiness to the lowest depth of misery, losing not only his property, but his children, and being himself afflicted with the worst sort of leprosy, but who, to the universal astonishment, was restored by God to health and happiness, suggested countless thoughts of the deepest human interest.

Ezekiel, as we have seen, mentions Enoch in one

place as the privileged possessor of superhuman wisdom. In another famous passage (Ezek. xiv., 14) he couples him with Noah and Job as an exceptionally righteous man, for the collocation "Noah, Daniel, and Job" is self-evidently wrong. There is no evidence that he perceived that greater suggestiveness in the story of Job of which I have spoken, and this blindness is not a feature in Ezekiel which draws us to the austere prophet. What was it that at last opened men's eyes? It was the continued disappointments of what is commonly called the post-exilic period. Post-exilic, indeed! Why, the Exile of Israel, in its deepest sense,* has lasted from Nebuchadrezzar's burning of Jerusalem to the present day. It is this that makes the Jews such idealists; it is this sense of exile which inspired that unknown "post-exilic" poet who gave the first adequate setting to the old Hebrew legend of Job the patient.

The Prologue (chaps. i. and ii.) and the Epilogue (xlii., 7–17) of the poem are both due to this writer. The former is full of delicate psychology and inimitable humour; the latter, which begins:

"And Jehovah said to Eliphaz the Temanite, My wrath is kindled against thee and thy two friends, because ye have not spoken of Me that which is right, as My servant Job has,"

* "In its deepest sense," *cf.* Lecture I., p. 12, "If there was a post-exilic age at all."

and ends with the statement that Job died having had his fill of life, is dry and prosaic,* and even morally, to us at least, disappointing. It was Job's high destiny, as we shall see, to " serve God for nought," and by having a tangible reward, as it were, forced upon him, he seems to us to be lowered in the moral scale. But to do justice to the writer we have to view him here not as an artist, but as a teacher. He cares for his people much more than for Job, and since a double compensation for Israel's calamities is a constant element in the later prophetic teaching, he feels bound to represent Job as having been amply compensated for his unmerited misfortunes. The chief value of the Epilogue is, that it enables us to reconstruct the main outlines of the omitted portion of the story. Thanks to it we are able, in some sense, to " call up him who left half told " (or whose editors have transmitted to us half told, or told amiss) the story of the most patient of men.

The result of an inquiry would probably be † that in lieu of Job iii.–xlii., 7, there stood originally something like this, only in a style of flowing, natural eloquence :

---

* Drs. Bartlett and Peters have from a literary point of view done well to omit the Epilogue in their excellent arrangement of select passages from the Bible (*Scriptures, Hebrew and Christian*, part vi., chap. v.).

† So first Macdonald, *Journal of Biblical Literature*, 1895, pp. 63–71.

"And these three men, moved at the sight of Job's grief, broke out into lamentations, and withheld not passionate complaints of the injustice of God. They said: Is there knowledge in the Most High? and does God judge righteous judgment? But Job was sore displeased, and reproved them, saying, Bitter is the pain which racks me, but more bitter still are the words which ye speak. Blessed be the Most High for that which He gave, and now that I am empty, blessed still be His name. I will call unto Him and say, Shew me wherein I have erred; let me not depart under the weight of Thine anger. For God is good to all those who call upon Him, and will not suffer the righteous to fall for ever. And Job reasoned ofttimes with his friends, and bade them repent, lest God should deal with them as with trangressors. And at the end of a season, God came to Eliphaz in a dream and said, My wrath is kindled against thee and thy two friends, because ye have not spoken of Me that which is right, as My servant Job has."

This, as it seems to me, is in harmony with the early view of Job as a perfectly righteous man—a second Abraham or Noah. It will account, too, for the severe blame which Jehovah gives to the three friends, and their liability to some mysterious punishment from which they can only be delivered by Job's intercession. Also for the high praise awarded to Job, who, as the poem now stands, certainly did not speak in all points rightly concerning God. Also for the expressions of another important work which appears to be based on the original Book of Job,—

I refer to the description of the suffering Servant of Jehovah in Isaiah lii., 13–liii., 12.

This noble description of the great Martyr, which has already enchanted us,* is in fact largely modelled on the original Book of Job. Reflecting on the cause of Job's misery, the writer came to the conclusion that God must have appointed this for the good of those who, unlike Job, were great transgressors, and that Job's consciousness of this must have helped him to bear his sufferings uncomplainingly. Such at any rate was his view respecting his own hero, the Servant of Jehovah. He does not deny that the Servant looked forward to his ultimate justification in public, but he evidently thinks that the really influential motive with the Servant was his ability through his sufferings to redeem his people from sin.† His hero does in fact serve God for nought. And this is certainly what the original poet of Job represented as the divine object in permitting the calamities which beset Job, viz., the demonstration by facts of the possibility of disinterested piety. It would be pleasant to think that the two writers were friends. We may at least conjecture that they were contemporaries, and that the writer of this Book of Job accepted the description

* See Lecture III.
† See Isa. liii., 10, 11, in *Polychrome Bible*.

of Jehovah's Servant as a kind of commentary on his own work.

Both these writers, I incline to think, lived after the introduction of Ezra's law-book; both are, at any rate, warmly attached to all existing religious institutions. Job is represented as an undoubting believer in sacrifices, and the Servant of Jehovah as commissioned to bring the true law of life to the nations. Neither of them can be moved from his rock-like faith in God by external privations. But by far the greater number of the Jews were incapable of this lofty piety. It was a fundamental tenet of the old Israelitish religion that all suffering was caused by some known or unknown offence against God, and the most that the ancient pre-exilic prophets could do was to stimulate men's consciences to discover those sins which, unrepented of, would bring great and deserved calamities on the community. It is true, they also preached the converse of this doctrine, viz., that by obeying the commands of God the community might ensure for itself His favour and protection. Morally, this preaching was of high value, even though it had little effect on the majority of its hearers. Its principal achievement was the production of the Book of Deuteronomy, which combines with a most thoughtful code of laws the oft-repeated assurance that obedience to Jehovah's precepts will be rewarded by prosperity, and deliberate disobedience punished by adversity and ruin. But again and again events occurred to falsify these assurances. The national adoption of Deuteronomy (in its original, simpler form) was followed by the disaster of Megiddo, and ultimately by the Captivities, and the introduction of Ezra's law-book was only an event in the domestic history of the Jews. On Nehemiah's departure, the rule of the Persians became less and less considerate, and the social abuses from which the community had always suffered so greatly, even if they were checked for a time, soon took a new lease of life. And, hence, that happy serenity which marks both Job (the original Job) and the Servant of Jehovah became as good as impossible. A Hebrew Pascal, the author of Psalm lxxiii., though he enriched theists with the noblest extant expression (to which I shall return*) of disinterested love to God, yet had to pass through a grievous experience of scepticism, and we need not therefore be surprised that one of the wise men of the close of the Persian, or more probably of the beginning of the Greek, period found the treatment of Job's sufferings by the original narrator inadequate for practical uses.

To this new writer it did not seem credible that

* See Lecture VI.

Job should have been unvisited by doubts respecting God's righteousness. Job, as the original story implied, was a symbol of the Jewish people, and even the best of the Jews had moments of painful scepticism, which it was as much as they could do to repress. Would not the Book of Job be more useful to the community if its hero were brought more into sympathy with ordinary Jewish feeling? In this way the patient Job became impatient. There was also another reason why this writer thought of altering the original conception of Job. He was evidently a cultivated man who had caught the "still sad music of humanity" in many walks of life. His interests were not confined to Judæa, and so, under his hands, Job became a symbol, not only of the Jewish people, but of humanity at large. Nor can one help seeing that this new writer was more of an individualist than his predecessor, *i. e.*, that he recognised the moral and religious rights of the individual as such, apart from the people to which he belonged. In the olden time, even a good man would not have expected to be as a matter of course prosperous, if he were a mere isolated unit in a community of bad men. But since Ezekiel had preached the doctrine that the son did not bear the iniquity of the father, nor the father the iniquity of the son, the old sense of solidarity began to give place to a new sense of the moral rights of the individual. The author of Job had, as I take it, learned to suffer and to sympathise with individuals. And the problem which presented itself to him was not merely, "Why does righteous Israel suffer?" but, "Why do righteous men everywhere suffer unjustly, and why, even if some punishment be deserved, is it so often disproportionate to the presumed moral cause?"

The consequence was that the rôles of Job and his friends were to some extent transposed. It was no longer, as in the original book, the three friends who spoke irreverently of the Most High, but Job himself. It is true, Job's hard speeches were drawn from him under extreme provocation, and are not to be interpreted in a cold, logical spirit. And strangely enough, to this bold Hebrew Prometheus comes at length a reconciling intuition of what may almost be called an Over-god, *i. e.*, of a God who loves and can be loved behind the God of pitiless and undiscriminating force. And this flash of insight comes to him (so the poet imagines, in accordance, doubtless, with his own experience) just when all earthly comfort appears to be denied him. At first, God seems deaf to his cry, and he turns for comfort to his friends. But the friends, under the chilling influence of the traditional doctrine of retribution, are driven to withhold sympathy from such a great sinner as they assume Job to be. Then, as the language of the friends becomes more violent, that of Job becomes calmer and more dignified. He begins to recognise what appears like a dual aspect in God. From the God of force, whom he sees in the countless sad phenomena of the world, he appeals to a God of love and sympathy, who is in heaven, and he becomes convinced that God will in some way do him justice. Almost he can believe that God will at length recall him from the nether world to which he is hastening; but he quickly dismisses the too seducing thought. This splendid passage I hope to quote later. But even if he be condemned by the strict laws of life and death to a perpetual imprisonment in Sheol, yet a divine testimony to his innocence is not impossible.

"O earth, cover not my blood,
And let my cry find no resting-place";

i. e., let not the earth absorb my unjustly shed blood, but, like Abel's, let it cry aloud for satisfaction. For, he continues:

"Even now, surely, my witness is in heaven,
And He that vouches for me is on high.
My flesh is athirst for God,
Towards Eloah mine eye drops tears,
That he would arbitrate for a man contending with God,
And between a mortal and his (divine) friend." *

* Job xvi., 18-21. (See *J. Q. R.*, Oct., 1897, pp. 14, 15.)

Later on, he expresses the same assured hope, and this time he connects it with the punishment of his friends. Bildad has just been forgetting himself so far as virtually to class Job with the wicked who know not God. This speech it is which brings on a crisis in Job's inward development. No longer can he tolerate the platitudes of his friends, which as applied to him are so cruelly unjust. He makes one more appeal, however, to their better feelings:

> " Have pity upon me, have pity upon me, O my friends,
>   For the hand of God has touched me.
>   Why do ye persecute me—like God,
>   And are never satiated with my flesh?" *

But he sees by their looks that his words fall idly on their ears. He longs that his words might be recorded in some permanent form—the words, that is, in which he asserts his innocence. But no sooner has he said this, than he bethinks himself of a far better justification which awaits him. It is the same idea of the divine Witness which we have already met with. But this time Job connects the idea with the punishment of his cruel friends. His appeal is not from the God of force to the God of love; for he is able by a new moral effort to reject once and for all the notion of a divided God. What he now de-

* Job xix., 21, 22.

sires is simply the vindication of his innocence, and the punishment of his cruel persecutors. He does not, indeed, understand God's treatment of him, but he no longer accuses God of injustice. It is his friends who are unjust, and they must be punished that his own justification may be complete:

> "But I know that my Avenger lives,
> And that at last He will appear above my grave;
> My Witness shall bring to pass my desire,
> And a curse will take hold of my foes.
>
> "My inner man is consumed with longing,
> For ye say, How (keenly) will we persecute him !
> Have terror because of the sword,
> For (God's) anger falls on the unjust." *

The crisis is past. Job's intellectual perplexity remains, but he does not doubt the existence of a moral God, though he cannot detect His operation:

> "I may go forward, but He is not there;
> And backward, but I cannot perceive Him." †

The friends, however, have learned nothing, and after hearing Job's reply to the third speech of Zophar—a reply which does not appear to have been preserved—we may presume that the earlier work ‡ recorded the departure of Job's false friends.

---

* Job xix., 25-29. (See the article in *J. Q. R.* already referred to.)
† Job, xxiii., 8.
‡ *I. e.*, that form of the poem which was intermediate between the original Book of Job and the book in its present form.

All that remained was to provide a suitable close for this great drama—a close which, if it settled nothing, should yet affirm once more that to be a sufferer was no proof of guilt. The poet's instinct guided him aright. He begins by charming us with a plaintive retrospect, by which Job seeks to cleanse his spirit from the bitterness of controversy (chaps. xxix., xxx.). Oh that those delicious days could be recalled, when the Almighty was his friend, and his children were about him! Then all at once he glides into a grand affirmation of his innocence (chap. xxxi.), which is one of the finest summaries of early Jewish morality, and finally passes from the scene with a marvellous piece of moral self-assertion which is nearly the most un-Hebraic passage in the whole of the Old Testament.

It was a truly noble specimen of didactic poetry, suffused with emotion, that this new poet produced. The problem of the cause of the suffering of the innocent was too big for him, but he set forth to the best advantage all the conflicting views of moralists known to him. He had at any rate succeeded (so he must have thought) in subverting the pernicious doctrine that from great sufferings we can argue the existence of great guilt. And he had represented Job as arriving finally at a state of resignation and of so much peace as was compatible with extreme perplexity on the intellectual question at issue. But he did not satisfy his fellow-philosophers any better than his predecessor had satisfied him. Various passages were inserted by later writers (for it is unnatural to suppose that the author was himself always changing), with the view of qualifying or counteracting parts of his work. These are of unequal value. The speeches of the youthful Elihu are inexpressibly poor, though not without value as a record of an age of intellectual decline. But I cannot help eulogising once more the noble Praise of Wisdom in chap. xxviii.—apart from the closing verse, which has converted it into a condemnation of free discussion. Nor can I refuse a still larger tribute of praise to the Speeches of Jehovah, which at first sight seem much too fine to be a later insertion. I am myself most willing to be convinced that the author of the Dialogues of the Friends had become discontented with his work, and appended the Speeches of Jehovah as a palinode. A purely literary critic can hardly help indulging in such a conjecture, but I fear that the canons of scientific criticism require us to reject it. The only safe view is, in my opinion, that some great poet—who thought the earlier Book of Job religiously imperfect—attached this appendix. The idea of the section is, that a minute criticism of the divine government (like that of Job) is as useless as contemplation of the wonders of nature is profitable. Job has to learn to forget himself in the glorious creation of which he forms a part. It is true, this is not directly stated. All that the poet says, by the mouth of Jehovah, is that Job had darkened the plan of the divine government by words devoid of insight (xxxviii., 2). The evident delight, however, which the poet takes in the pictures of creation justifies us in supposing that he recommends the contemplation of nature as a remedy against painful and futile scepticism. Whatever we may think of his attitude towards free thought, he has given us a splendid literary record of one of the early stages of the love of the higher Wisdom among the Jews, and we may be thankful that it has found so prominent and honourable a place in the Biblical Literature.

LECTURE V.

Orthodox and Heretical Wisdom; Contemporary Levitical Piety.

IT will hardly be denied that Jewish religion owes a debt of gratitude to Babylon and Persia. Not only a wholesome religious stimulus, but some easily assimilated ideas and beliefs came to it from these sources. I am afraid that we cannot speak as favourably of the first contact between Jewish and Greek thought. A most uncongenial spirit of doubt now begins to be traceable in Judaism. The Book of Proverbs itself—that carefully prepared handbook of popular religious instruction—contains at least one passage (Prov. xxx., 2-4) directly antithetical to the devout eulogy of Wisdom in Prov. viii. Here is this unique sceptical poem. It takes us back to a time before any product of the Wisdom-Literature was a holy Scripture, and the remarkable thing is that it has been interwoven with a very different passage, which has the nature of an antidote. It is in two stanzas of six lines each, and this, if I read it correctly, is the heading prefixed to it: "The

Words of Agur ben Jakeh the Poet." Whether this is the author's real name or a pseudonym, I cannot tell.

" A solemn speech of the man whose inquiry was for God:
I have inquired for God, but have had no success.
For I have less sense than other men,
And there is in me no human understanding ;
Neither have I learned wisdom,
So that I might obtain the knowledge of the holy ones.

" Who can go up to heaven and come down ?
Who can gather the wind in his fists ?
Who can bind the waters in a garment ?
Who can grasp all the ends of the earth ?
(Such an one would I question thus about God),
   What is His name ?
And what is the name of His sons, if thou knowest it ? "

Such is my view of the poem. The speaker is a Jew, but with a strong dash of the Greek or modern spirit. He is a prototype of Goethe's Faust. You know those fine lines which the German poet puts into the mouth of his hero, and which Bayard Taylor has so finely translated :

  " Who dare express Him ?
  And who profess Him ?
  Saying, 'I believe in Him !'
  Who, feeling, seeing,
  Deny His being,
  Saying, 'I believe Him not !'
  The All-enfolding,

> The All-upholding,
> Folds and upholds He not
> Thee, me, Himself?
> Arches not then the sky above us?
> Lies not beneath us, firm, the earth?
> And rise not, on us shining,
> Friendly, the everlasting stars?
>
> . . . .
>
> I have no name to give it!
> Feeling is all in all;
> The name is sound and smoke,
> Obscuring Heaven's clear glow." *

It may be something akin to this, only with less of sentiment and theory, that the Hebrew poet means. He has heard fine things said about God as the Creator and Governor of the world; and various names and titles have been given to this great Being,—Yahwè, for instance (so the too familiar Jehovah should be corrected), Adonai, Elohim, El Shaddai, Yahwè Sebaoth, God the Mighty One, Shepherd of Israel. Which of these is the right name—the name which correctly expresses the divine nature or character, and which within the compass of a few letters sums up the Infinite One? The poet has also heard, in favourite narratives and in temple-hymns, of the "sons of God"—a phrase which seems to him hardly in accordance with those transcendental views of the divine nature which have rightly taken the

* *Goethe's Faust*, by Bayard Taylor, i., 191 *f.*

scepticism is perfectly natural. But you must remember that we are now in the Greek period, and if in the *Rig Veda* we find such an expression of honest scepticism as that which I am about to quote, why should we be surprised that the same characteristically Aryan spirit should have spread from the conquering Greeks to the conquered Jews? "Who knows?" says the unnamed Sanscrit poet,—

"Who knows, who here can declare, whence has sprung—whence, this creation? . . . From what this creation arose, and whether (any one) made it, or not, he who in the highest heaven is its ruler, he verily knows, or (even) he does not know." *

At a later period (second century A.D.) the sceptical poet Agur might seem to have risen from the dead in the person of Elisha ben Abuyah, who became such a deep theosophist that he fell away from revealed religion,† or, as Jewish writers say, penetrated into Paradise, and destroyed the plants which grow there—a delightful figure, is it not? and greatly to be preferred to more abstract phraseology. The Rabbis speak with pain of Elisha's apostacy, and give their lost leader the name of Acher, "a stranger, one who is not of us."

---

* Muir, *Ancient Sanscrit Texts*, v., 356.

† We are informed that he was strengthened in his irreligion by observing the hard trials of those who practised the Law, and who notwithstanding rested their hopes of happiness on their legal righteousness.

It seems almost miraculous that this strange sceptical poem of Agur should have been safely conveyed to the modern world. This would certainly not have occurred but for the pious protest in which it was embalmed. It is to this protest of orthodoxy that I now ask your attention.

The writer of the protest begins by declaring his faith in divine revelation. He says:

" Every saying of God is free from dross ;
　He is a shield to all those who take refuge in Him."

That is, the purest wisdom is to be found in God's Book. The proof of this is the protection enjoyed by those who trust in God. Piety and its rewards are, it is implied, confined to those who take every statement in the Bible to be authoritative. Then he continues:

" See thou add not to His words,
　Lest He convict thee and thou be proved a liar."

That is, what has not been revealed is not true. The freethinker, who puts the title "solemn speech" at the head of his poem as if it were a prophecy, will have to suffer some calamity.

" Two things I ask of Thee;
　Withhold them not from me, before I die.
　Levity and the speech (of folly
　And) lying do Thou put far from me.

> Be my lot neither poverty nor riches,
> Feed me with the bread which is my share;
> Else if I were full, I might become a denier,
> And say, Who is Jehovah?
> Or if I were impoverished, I might be so robbed of understanding
> As to treat profanely the name of my God." *

These two petitions are in reality but one. It is the poet Agur to whom this worthy man alludes—Agur, who had professed not to know the right name of God, and whom the orthodox protester may perhaps have supposed to have denied that there was any Being, even in heaven, who could bind the waters, and gather the wind. In short, the champion of orthodoxy asks that he may not become like Agur. He sees that if he were at either extreme of society he might be tempted to deny the God of Israel, for the rich man appears not to need God, and the poor man seems to be forsaken by Him. He therefore declines riches—a somewhat remarkable phenomenon; the other wise men are obviously far enough from doing so. It is true, this wise man is partly influenced by a wish to counteract the words of Agur; perhaps if put to the test he might have found riches not wholly undesirable.

The other proverbial poems of Agur, contained in the same chapter of Proverbs, do not concern us.

* Prov. xxx., 5–9.

It is enough that we have found a stray specimen of a literature of scepticism. I do not hesitate to use this expression, for such a poem cannot have stood alone. Homer tells us indeed that there was only one Thersites in the Greek army before Troy. Fortunate Achilles and Agamemnon! There were certainly not a few Agurs at Jerusalem from the third century B.C. onwards. Evidence of this is supplied by a work of a very different school—the Book of Enoch. The passage which I shall quote belongs to the earliest part of this book:

"And now I know this mystery, that many sinners will alter and pervert the words of uprightness, and will speak wicked words, and lie, and practise great deceits, and write books concerning their words." *

The supposed speaker is one of the very persons to whom Agur probably alludes when he says, "Who has gone up to heaven and come down?"— the patriarch Enoch. But his words are those of a writer of the age of John Hyrcanus, who reigned from 135 to 105 B.C. And the statement is confirmed by the editorial appendix to one of the latest writings in the Old Testament, where there seems to be an emphatic caution against philosophical books of a more "advanced" character than those

* Enoch civ., 10 (Charles's ed., p. 299).

Be my lot neither poverty nor riches,
Feed me with the bread which is my share;
Else if I were full, I might become a denier,
And say, Who is Jehovah?
Or if I were impoverished, I might be so robbed of understanding
As to treat profanely the name of my God."*

These two petitions are in reality but one. It is the poet Agur to whom this worthy man alludes— Agur, who had professed not to know the right name of God, and whom the orthodox protester may perhaps have supposed to have denied that there was any Being, even in heaven, who could bind the waters, and gather the wind. In short, the champion of orthodoxy asks that he may not become like Agur. He sees that if he were at either extreme of society he might be tempted to deny the God of Israel, for the rich man appears not to need God, and the poor man seems to be forsaken by Him. He therefore declines riches—a somewhat remarkable phenomenon; the other wise men are obviously far enough from doing so. It is true, this wise man is partly influenced by a wish to counteract the words of Agur; perhaps if put to the test he might have found riches not wholly undesirable.

The other proverbial poems of Agur, contained in the same chapter of Proverbs, do not concern us.

* Prov. xxx., 5–9.

It is enough that we have found a stray specimen of a literature of scepticism. I do not hesitate to use this expression, for such a poem cannot have stood alone. Homer tells us indeed that there was only one Thersites in the Greek army before Troy. Fortunate Achilles and Agamemnon! There were certainly not a few Agurs at Jerusalem from the third century B.C. onwards. Evidence of this is supplied by a work of a very different school—the Book of Enoch. The passage which I shall quote belongs to the earliest part of this book:

"And now I know this mystery, that many sinners will alter and pervert the words of uprightness, and will speak wicked words, and lie, and practise great deceits, and write books concerning their words." *

The supposed speaker is one of the very persons to whom Agur probably alludes when he says, "Who has gone up to heaven and come down?"— the patriarch Enoch. But his words are those of a writer of the age of John Hyrcanus, who reigned from 135 to 105 B.C. And the statement is confirmed by the editorial appendix to one of the latest writings in the Old Testament, where there seems to be an emphatic caution against philosophical books of a more "advanced" character than those

* Enoch civ., 10 (Charles's ed., p. 299).

sanctioned in the Canon. I will read a passage from this appendix:

"The words of the wise are as goads, and as nails firmly driven in. They were written down [*i. e.*, edited] by framers of collections, but were given by another teacher.* And as to all besides these, my son, be on thy guard. Of making many books there is no end, and too much reading fatigues the body." †

This short, condensed style is in the manner of the later Jewish writers, who make large demands on the intelligence of their readers. The passage seems to mean this: "Sayings of wise men, like those in Proverbs and Ecclesiastes, are highly to be recommended, for they stimulate the mind and do not burden the memory. They have no doubt been edited by authorised persons, but they were originally produced, in each case, by a teacher distinct from the editors. They may be read with confidence; there is no legitimate requirement which they do not satisfy. But there are also many other literary products in circulation. I warn my disciples to be on their guard against these. No good, but much useless fatigue, is to be got from reading them." The books to which the epilogue containing these cautions is attached are Proverbs (which includes the fragments of the poems

* This view of the text, however, is only probable.
† Eccles. xii., 11, 12.

Orthodox and Heretical Wisdom 183

of Agur) and Ecclesiastes. These are pronounced not too "advanced" for faithful Israelites to read.

It is Ecclesiastes which now beckons us,—that most singular book which Heinrich Heine called the Song of Songs of Scepticism, and Franz Delitzsch, by a doubtful correction, the Song of Songs of Religion. It is quite impossible to do justice to my subject without some reference to Ecclesiastes, though, unfortunately, I must add that this is one of the most difficult books to comprehend in the form in which it has come down to us. The inconsistencies which the book presents are much more startling than we can readily account for on the assumption of its integrity. The inconsistencies of Montaigne are those of an open and a growing mind; those of Ecclesiastes are such as cannot exist together in a rational thinker. I admit that very similar inconsistencies exist in the Book of Job, and that if we have been able to convince ourselves of the unity of the Book of Job we may not find it impossible to defend the integrity of Ecclesiastes. If, however, we have found the Book of Job to be a monument, not of one, but of two or three conflicting schools, we shall be prepared to find more than one school represented in Ecclesiastes, and if the contents of Ecclesiastes, apart from certain perfectly orthodox passages, are more startling than even the hardest parts of Job, we shall be prepared to find that still more violent means were taken to mitigate the shock which Ecclesiastes gave to the reader. Lastly, if in later times both Proverbs and the Song of Songs were ascribed to Solomon, we shall not be surprised if, after the Book of Ecclesiastes had been made theologically sound, another late writer should have made it subservient to the legend of Solomon's repentance. These three things have, as I believe, come to pass. Ecclesiastes has been interpolated in an orthodox interest.* Either accident or violence has almost entirely destroyed the connection; and the speaker, Koheleth (our Bible renders, "the Preacher"; the name denotes a representative of the class of public preachers, without reference to any individual), has actually been identified with Solomon—a step which has naturally involved fresh interpolations. It is an extremely difficult task to recover conjecturally the original order of the sayings. It seems to me as if passages had been omitted as well as inserted, and I do not feel at all sure that Gustav Bickell in his restoration has not been rather too anxious to produce a perfect treatise of Hebrew philosophy. According to this Roman

---

* This is not a new view. The objections which have been offered to it appear to the present writer to have no cogency. To discuss the question adequately would only be possible in a commentary on Ecclesiastes, written from an "advanced" critical point of view, in which the interpolations would be pointed out.

Catholic scholar, the true Ecclesiastes is a carefully thought-out answer to a question familiar enough to ourselves,—Is life worth living? He makes it fall into two parts,—a critical-speculative and a practical-ethical part, the former showing that supposed absolute goods (everything which a man has, or knows, or can do) are resultless and unsatisfying, the latter recommending, as at least relatively good, wisdom and the cheerful enjoyment of life.

It would hardly be safe to adopt this theory, and the more so as another reconstruction may soon be hoped for from America.* All that I lay stress upon is the great probability that the present disorder in the contents of the book did not originally exist. The author was certainly, considering the gloominess of his time, not a contemptible writer. The tact with which he introduces occasional pieces of metrical verse is one indication of this. It is not likely that he would have turned out so unequal a piece of work as our present Ecclesiastes, and done so much injustice to his argument. Gladly would I continue this subject, but I must not be tempted away from my main object, which is to ascertain how much religion the author had. I will quote his finest bit of writing later on.

* It will form part of the *Polychrome Bible;* Professor Haupt is the author.

That he has warm and deep feelings is plain at a glance, and a careful reading will show that he has also a religion—he is neither practically nor theoretically an atheist. But compare the God in whom he believes with the Jehovah of the psalmists, and oh, the difference! That he never names the name Yahwè or Jehovah is a trifle; the misery is that his God is so far removed from the earth, and so unsympathetic. He is one whom it is wise to fear and to obey, even if no reward for obedience can be reckoned upon, but whom it is not easy to love, and impossible in any sense to comprehend.* Long ago this God has predestinated † all that shall happen; prudence therefore bids us fold our arms and acquiesce in the inevitable. So, then, to the most fundamental tenet of the earlier Judaism, the belief in one God, the author clings; it gives him no joy, no rapture, but it saves him from the gulf of waters. On the other hand, he has abandoned (and so doubtless has Agur, the freethinker) a tenet only less fundamental—that of a proportionate retribution upon earth for the righteous and the wicked, and even refuses the sweet anodyne, accepted by most Jews, of a great reckoning-day in the future, when there will be a separation between the righteous and the wicked, between him who serves God and him who

* Eccles. viii., 17. † Eccles. vi., 10.

serves Him not. I will not say that the author anywhere denies that God does sometimes punish the sinner. But of anything like a principle of retributive justice in the divine government he can see no trace. He says with much bitterness:

"There is many a righteous man who perishes in spite of his righteousness, and many a wicked man who lives long in spite of his wickedness."*

And again:

"There is a vanity (a disappointment or disillusionment) which happens on the earth, viz., that there are righteous men who fare according to the work of the wicked, and that there are wicked men who fare according to the work of the righteous. I say that this also is vanity." †

Such statements, unsoftened by any reference to a final judgment, gave great pain to the devout. They feared for the young readers who might be charmed by the boldness of the author, and led into the devious paths of heterodoxy. Recourse was therefore had by pious editors to the expedient of interpolation. A considerable degree of success was obtained. In the Epilogue the author was described as a simply devout man, and in the body of the work he was made to confess that the wicked were really punished here, and would be punished here-

* Eccles. vii., 15. † Eccles. viii., 14.

after. Later on, the popular paraphrase called the Targum went a great deal farther, adapting the book to the fully developed eschatology of later Judaism. But when you have before you an Ecclesiastes in which the results of criticism are indicated, you will, I think, see that there are only two undoubtedly original passages in which the moral practice and the outward fortunes of men are brought into any kind of relation. I will quote and explain these passages. One of them reads thus:

"Be not overmuch wicked, neither be thou foolish; why shouldest thou die before thy time?"*

The other is:

"When thou hast vowed a vow unto God, defer not the payment. Suffer not thy mouth to bring punishment on thy body, neither say thou before the messenger, It was spoken rashly; why should God be angry at thy voice, and destroy the work of thy hands?"†

The first of these passages seems to say that there are certain extremely wicked acts which exhaust the long-suffering of God, and bring the surest punishment on the offender. But this can hardly be the true meaning, for a companion saying exists, not less remarkably expressed:

"Be not righteous overmuch, neither make thyself overwise; why shouldest thou destroy thyself?"‡

* Eccles. vii., 17 (Authorised Version).
† Eccles. v., 4, 6 (new translation).
‡ Eccles. vii., 16 (Authorised Version).

Clearly this cannot mean that those who make righteousness and wisdom their chief concern are displeasing to God. The two sayings must have been framed from a practical man's point of view, and the terms " righteous" and "wicked " must be taken as they were commonly understood in the religious world, *i. e.*, in a Pharisæan sense. Righteousness, then, denotes the observance, and wickedness the neglect, of the more minute details of the Law. To carry legal obedience to the point of asceticism was not less suicidal than to allow a sense of superiority to such pedantry to tempt a man into sensual licence. In both cases the punishment referred to is simply that which arises from the transgression of natural laws. He who is at once moderately pious and moderately worldly will, according to Koheleth, be a truly wise man.

The second passage seems to show that even this rationalist thinker was not completely emancipated from traditional scruples. One offence there was which would not escape punishment, and that was, to vow and not to pay the vow. If you do this, says the author, you will have to suffer in your person, and when you tell the priest's messenger that you spoke the vow inconsiderately, it is not he, but God, who will be irritated, and who will punish you with the loss of property. So the very man who does not believe in the Messiah, believes in a divine vengeance for unfulfilled vows!

One cannot help pitying our author. Of course his conscience bade him disbelieve in the judgment, and yet he could ill afford to do so. I do not deny that there were Jews in that age who were as capable as St. Bernard of disinterested love of God. For instance, there was the great teacher Antigonus of Soco, who said, "Be not as slaves that serve with a view to recompense; but be as those who serve disinterestedly, and let the fear of Heaven [*i.e.*, God] be upon you." It is true he uses the word "fear," but what he means is reverent love. We must remember, however, that Antigonus was a disciple of Simeon the Righteous, whose characteristic saying he must be considered to presuppose. The saying of Simeon the Righteous ran thus:

"The world rests on three things—on the Law, on the services of worship, and on acts of loving-kindness."

If the author of Ecclesiastes had been as devoted to the Law and to the forms of worship as Antigonus of Soco,—if he had regarded them as absolute goods, the following of which was its own reward,—he might have safely abandoned the Messianic hope. But this was certainly not the case. He believed in no absolute goods, was no enthusiast even for the Law, and thought it necessary to deprecate excessive piety. Less than other men, therefore, could he with impunity abandon the belief in God's retributive justice. If, indeed, he had accepted a certain new doctrine, just beginning to be popular,—that of Immortality, —all might have been well. But no one could prove to his satisfaction that the spirit of man went upward, and that it was only the spirit of the beasts which went downward to the earth.* The wonder is that he could maintain such morality and such a belief in God as he had. " Fear thou God," † he says with all earnestness. If he recommends the pleasures of the table, he does so with a sad irony; enjoy at any rate these pleasures, he says, because they have not the painful consequences of higher pleasures, and because the time for enjoying them is so short; besides,— he strangely adds,—they are the gift of God. For himself, it is true, they have long lost their savour. But youth will be youth, and he does not grudge the young men, for whom he especially writes, a chance of trying these pleasures before they pronounce them mere apples of Sodom.

He also dwells strongly on the happiness of a pure wedlock. His sincerity in this is beyond all doubt. And here, at least, he is a true Jew; here, at least, he shows his aversion to one of the most

* Eccles. iii., 21. † Eccles. v., 7.

characteristic vices of Hellenism. That he has himself had a bad experience of women,* and has apparently missed that prize which is "above rubies," does not make him grudge a better fortune to others. Enjoy life, he says, with a woman whom thou lovest, all thy fleeting days †; and again:

> "Give no place to sorrow in thy mind,
> From thy body keep trouble afar;
> Of thy cistern take good heed
> In the days of youthful age." ‡

What "cistern" means in a Semitic poem is well expressed by Mr. Lyall in a note to one of his translations of old Arabic poetry: "The 'cistern' is a man's home and family, and whatever he holds dear."

To those of riper age our author speaks in more subdued tones:

> "Better to go to the house of mourning
> Than to go to the house of feasting.
> For there is the end of all,
> The living will take it to heart.
> Better is sorrow than laughter,
> With a gloomy face the heart is cheerful." §

I cannot feel sure, however, that the author practised

---

* Eccles. vii., 27, 28.
† Eccles. viii., 9.
‡ Eccles. xi., 10a, xii., 1a; cf. Cheyne, *Job and Solomon*, pp. 227, 300.
§ Eccles. vii., 2, 3.

his own advice to visit mourners. Had he done so, we should surely have heard something of the duty of showing practical sympathy to the distressed. He evidently had a true sense of the misery of mankind, but it does not appear that he troubled himself much about the misery of individuals. The writers of the Book of Proverbs are not open to this criticism. For instance, one of them says, speaking of some outrage on humanity :

"Deliver those who are being taken to death,
  And those who go with tottering steps to be slain, hold thou back." *

But I am afraid that under such circumstances our author would have been content with looking sadly on, and saying with a groan, " This also is vanity." Perhaps he may be excused on account of his advanced age, or perhaps it is his theory of life which has weakened his benevolent impulses. For he tells us :

"I have seen all the works that are done under the sun ; and behold, all is vanity and vexation of spirit. That which is crooked cannot be made straight, and a deficit cannot be reckoned in." †

And then we meet with this remarkable confession of ineradicable egoism :

* Prov. xxiv., 11.   † Eccles. i., 14, 15.

"And I hated all my toil which I had performed under the sun, because I shall have to leave the fruits of it to one who will come after me. And who knows whether he will be a wise man or a fool? And he will rule over all that I have gained with toil and wisdom under the sun; this also is vanity." *

No thought enters his head of lending his money to Jehovah, as the proverb-writers said,† or of giving all his goods to build schools and found hospitals; and it is characteristic of the poverty of his book from a philanthropic point of view that a passage which in reality is simply an exhortation to bold business enterprise ("Send thy bread upon the waters, for thou shalt find it after many days"), has been converted by preachers into a recommendation of beneficence. The truth is that the unhappy author has but a weak social sense. From old habit and the influence of his orthodox education he may act in many things like any ordinary Jew, but the bond of Jewish nationality exercises almost no inward force upon him, and he has not gained that new sense of the solidarity of mankind which is so powerfully expressed by the great Stoic Roman emperor. Mankind is to him only an aggregate of millions of worthless atoms. Happier, far happier, were Saul and Ahab, and many another who sacri-

* Eccles. ii., 18, 19. † Prov. xix., 17.

ficed his life for his people, not hoping to receive it again, than this melancholy egoist, who had in him no doubt the germs of fine qualities, but whose development had been rudely interrupted by an excessive deference to the spirit of scepticism. Certainly he was not a bad man, and yet there must have been a weakness in his moral fibre; otherwise his Jewish feeling would have been keener, and his opposition to complete pessimism more effective. There must also, one thinks, have been some defect in his intellectual capacity; else he would have been drawn irresistibly either to the Hebrew-Persian doctrine of the Resurrection, or to the newer Greek doctrine of the Immortality of the Soul. Either of these tenets would have saved him from spiritual famine, and have enabled him to carry on the work so usefully begun by successive writers in that noble composite poem, the Book of Job.

No wonder that opinions were much divided about this extraordinary book. Many were repelled, but almost as many (I suppose) were attracted by it. Doubters are always grateful to the writer who can give vigorous and, to some extent, artistic expression to the thoughts which stir within them. That there was much scepticism among the Jews in the later post-exilic period is certain, though, naturally enough, the evidence for this is scanty. The overthrow of the Persian Empire by Alexander was of itself a fruitful source of religious doubt. Long had that empire been tottering to its fall, and the Jews had comforted themselves for their manifold miseries by the thought that when the fall came the restored kingdom of Israel would come too. But it came not, and some men began to think that fortune was on the side of Greek power, and truth on that of Greek philosophy. Even the Maccabæan revolution did not succeed in extinguishing the sceptical tendency. The extreme Hellenisers, who would have substituted Zeus for Jehovah, were no doubt swept away by it. But the improvement in Jewish circumstances was not such as to render religious doubt impossible. The old doctrine of retribution and the newer Messianic hope were equally hard to reconcile with facts, and the increasing knowledge of the world made the narrowness of Jewish orthodoxy more and more unpalatable to many thinkers. To such persons the deeply felt and vigorously expressed scepticism of Ecclesiastes appealed with great force. To suppress the book was impossible. All that the religious authorities could do was to neutralise its teaching. This they effected (as we have seen), partly by shuffling up certain sections, and so destroying the connection, and partly by interpolating passages referring to the future judgment and to the *blasé* and penitent King Solomon. To us the Solomonic reference is shocking in the extreme, but an earlier age (probably) had already seen equally startling transformations of history in the Books of Chronicles. The Epilogue, too, received this remarkable appendix:

" The final result, all having been heard : Fear God, and keep His commandments, for this is the whole (duty) of man. For every work will God bring into the judgment (which will be) upon all that is concealed and all that is manifest, whether it be good or evil."*

Thus the author was made the preacher of a doctrine in which he did not believe, and a pillar of an orthodoxy which he had tried and found wanting. He even became idealised into a penitent, backsliding king, and under cover of that king's name his book made its way into the Canon.

And now as to the date of the book. We know, of course, that it is a post-exilic work; no critic would hesitate to use it in a historical sketch like the present. But to what part of the post-exilic period does it belong? The question is of much interest, and presses for an answer. That the spirit and tendency of the book presuppose Greek philosophical influence is sufficiently clear. Take the first autobiographical passage; of course I omit the

* Eccles. xii., 13, 14.

interpolated words "was [or, have been] king over Israel in Jerusalem."

"I Koheleth (or, the Preacher) gave my mind to making search and exploration, by wisdom, concerning all that is done under heaven; it is sore trouble which God has given to the human race to undergo. I saw all works which are done under the sun."*

This means that Koheleth is, or would like to be, a critical inquirer into the condition of humanity. Can there be anything more un-Hebraic, more un-Oriental, than the idea, unless, indeed, it be the form of expression? And what unsophisticated Hebrew writer could possibly have understood this saying:

"Also He has put the world into their mind, except that man cannot find out from beginning to end the work which God has made"?†

Certain passages suggest the possibility that the author had a leaning to Stoicism. Just so, the saying of Antigonus of Soco (quoted elsewhere) on disinterested obedience may seem to have Stoic affinities. Nor is it inconceivable that the ideas of other philosophical schools may have filtered down to our author. It would be dangerous, however, to speak positively on this subject, because of the

* Eccles. i., 12-14.
† Eccles. iii., 11. See Cheyne, *Job and Solomon*, p. 210.

want of undeniably technical philosophical terms in the Hebrew text of Ecclesiastes. Indirect Greek philosophical influence is all that is quite certain.

It is at any rate something to know that our author's date is subsequent to the conquests of Alexander. On linguistic grounds he must, it would seem, have written later than 290 B.C., the earliest date which anyone has proposed for the Book of Ecclesiasticus, and if so, since neither the Maccabæan rising nor the preceding period provides a suitable background, we cannot stop short till we come to the time of John Hyrcanus (135-105 B.C.). To this period Ecclesiastes has been assigned by Renan. The objection is twofold: First, the reign of Hyrcanus was a brilliant one, and made most Jews feel proud of their country.* And next, though Hyrcanus had the royal power, he contented himself with the title of high priest. The reign of Alexander Jannæus (104-78 B.C.), a son of John Hyrcanus, comes next into consideration. It was a period of miserable civil wars, and the doings of the King were such as to alienate all high-minded Jews. It was also a period when Greek influence was very strong; Josephus tells us that the King's brother and predecessor, Aristobulus, bore the title

* We see this from a remarkable passage in pseudo-Jonathan's Targum on Deut. xxxiii., 11.

of Philhellen. But how strange it would be if a book written at this period gave no indication of the strife which then raged between the Sadducees and the Pharisees! Let us go a little farther down, and read Josephus's account of the reign of Herod, miscalled the Great. It was a time, he tells us, of general terror and insecurity. The citizens of Jerusalem dared not even walk or eat together, because the tyrant had forbidden all social gatherings. Spies were set everywhere, both in and near the city; Herod himself, it is said, mingled in disguise with the people, not, like a famous caliph, to find out whether they were happy,* but to catch up expressions of discontent. His avowed and irreconcilable adversaries he persecuted, and if they protested he took their lives. A general oath of allegiance was imposed, from which only the Essenes, to whom Herod was partial, were excused. Above 6000 Pharisees refused the oath, and were fined; some of them were afterwards revengefully slain.† I confess that I can at present find no period which so adequately explains the allusions in Ecclesiastes as this. Can we not see that the chief source of the misery described in it is the general sense of danger? Listen to this advice of the author:

* The story of Haroun-al-Rashid is legendary, however.
† Jos., *Ant.*, xv., 10, 4; xvii., 2, 4.

"Curse not the king, even on thy couch,
And curse not the rich in thy bedchamber,
For the birds of the air may carry the sound,
And the winged ones report the speech."*

He tells us, too, that this suspicious ruler is no high-born personage, but has the tyrannical instincts of a *parvenu*:

"Woe to thee, O land, when thy king is a servant!
Happy art thou, O land, when thou hast a king who was born free." †

Singularly enough, there is a Talmudic legend ‡ which makes a distinguished Rabbi, deprived of his sight by Herod, quote these very passages in an interview with the King. I should mention that Herod had put on a disguise, and was seeking to tempt the Rabbi to speak bitter words against the man who had blinded him. The story belongs to a class of narratives which are obviously unhistorical, but at least shows the feeling of a later age that the tyranny of Herod was most fitly illustrated by Ecclesiastes.

The whole book may be explained from this point of view, and it will become truly alive. For in-

---
* Eccles. x., 20. "Bedchamber" is a necessary correction.

† Eccles. x., 16a, 17a. The passage quoted reminds us of Isa. iii., 4; the unquoted portion, of Isa. v., 11. The writer finds in these prophetic passages an applicability to his own times.

‡ *Baba Bathra*, 4a. Usually this story is treated as historical. But see the remark at the close of this paragraph.

stance, why does the writer compassionate a land whose king is a servant? Because Herod belonged to a race which had been lately subjugated by the Jews, and even compelled to change its religion. In the Talmud he actually receives the title "slave of the Asmonæan house," reminding us of Ecclesiastes, because the Idumæans had been conquered by John Hyrcanus. Compare this passage too:

"I saw slaves on horseback, and princes (walking) like slaves on the ground." *

The meaning of this may be that Herod dispossessed the Asmonæans and their friends, and put his own partisans (*parvenus* and perhaps Idumæans) into all the best posts. And here is another striking allusion to politics:

" Be not involved in a bad affair;
For he can do all that he wills;
Because the word of the king is decisive;
Who can ask, What doest thou?" †

Do we not feel the heavy air of the despotism of Herod? Experience has warned the writer of the fatal consequences of being involved in revolutionary attempts. Listen again:

" The wise man observes the king's commandment
Because of the oath by God." ‡

* Eccles. x., 7. † Eccles. viii., 3, 4; *cf*. x., 4.
‡ Eccles. viii., 2 (following Bickell).

This seems to allude to the compulsory oath of which Josephus has told us. A similar allusion is perhaps traceable in the following passage:

" There is one and the same fate for every one, for the righteous and the wicked, for the clean and for the unclean, for the sacrificer and for the non-sacrificer. The good man fares just like the sinner, and he that swears as he that fears an oath." *

Here there seems to be a reference to the Essenes, who, as Josephus asserts, refrained from the usual sacrifices, having purer lustrations of their own, and forbade swearing, because a man whose simple affirmation could not be trusted was condemned already. Fortunately for them Herod respected their scruple about swearing. But our author evidently depreciates the class of non-swearers. Presumably he includes the Essenes (who also, be it remembered, rejected matrimony) among the " ultra-religious " people who, as he forcibly says, " destroyed themselves."

There is a description of Essene asceticism in the Book of Enoch,† which, though written from a very different point of view, confirms the opinion here adopted, viz., that the author of Ecclesiastes makes allusions to the Essenes. In it these self-denying men are represented as loving heaven more than

* Eccles. ix., 2.   † Enoch cviii. ; cf. cii.

their worldly life, and are contrasted with the sinners who deny judgment and resurrection. The antithesis between Ecclesiastes and Enoch is complete.*

We need not be surprised at this wide divergence between the writers of the two books. The one gives us the dry light of experience and philosophy; the other irradiates the facts of life with the light of visions and dreams. The one believes in the divine guidance of the fortunes of Israel; the other has lost almost all sense of nationality without having gained the greater citizenship of the world. The writer in Enoch is in spirit, if not in fact, an Essene; the author of Ecclesiastes would sympathise more with the Sadducees than with any other of the leading schools of thought. Thus we have in their respective writings, monuments of two of the three great tendencies of later Judaism. I do not, of course, say that the writer of Ecclesiastes was a typical Sadducee. Probably Ben Sira—the wise man who composed Ecclesiasticus—was closer to the ordinary Sadducæan type, alike in his sacerdotalism and in his theology.† But there was, I suppose,

* *Cf.* Lecture VI.

† This is confirmed by the fact that the Books of the Sadducees and the Book of Ben Sira are placed side by side on the old Jewish Index Expurgatorius. See *Sanhedrin*, 100b; Taylor, *Jewish Fathers*, p. 129.

room in the great Sadducæan party for men of differing degrees of culture and conservatism. I may add that in the so-called Psalms of Solomon (see Lecture VI.) we have an undoubted record of the religion of the Pharisees. It is well that we should learn to know every school or party from its own ablest representatives, and so students may be advised to read these books, which cannot fail to correct the bias with which, if their education has been Christian, they not unnaturally approach New Testament times.

It is possible, no doubt, that we may have less religious sympathy with Ecclesiastes than with the other two books, and I am quite certain that looking back on the Book of Job and even on those of Proverbs and Ecclesiasticus, we shall feel disappointed at the apparent failure of the great movement towards Wisdom. But let us remember that the writer with whom religiously we sympathise least is the one with whom on other grounds we cannot help sympathising most. His frankness and the width of his outlook both charm us, and, when we recollect the miserable age in which he lived, our criticism of his religious deficiencies gives place to the sincerest pity. He might, no doubt, have saved his religious fervour by joining the Pharisees or the Essenes. But to have done so he would have had to sacrifice the conception of a broad human culture which he had gained from Greece. It was needful that the attempt should be made to engraft this conception on Jewish thought, and so to combine Jewish theism with Hellenic rationalism. The first to make this attempt suffered for his boldness, but we, who pity but who do not dare to censure the atrophy of certain parts of his higher nature (similar to that which, by his own admission, was suffered by the illustrious Darwin), cannot withhold our appreciation of the noble though unsuccessful endeavour of the writer of Ecclesiastes.

For, after all, it would have been an immense misfortune if Jewish theism had become absolutely and permanently committed to Pharisaism. Later on, the Jewish people in Palestine was indeed virtually captured by Pharisaism, but the existence of Ecclesiastes in the Canon, even in its manipulated form, was a protest against this, and unless the world were to continue divided into Jews and non-Jews it was necessary that the attempt to Hellenise Jewish religion should be renewed. What attitude our philosophic Sadducee would have adopted towards such a renewal, it is useless to surmise. But one may justly suppose that his outlook would have been far less pessimistic, and that some elementary form of the idea of progress would have compensated him for the renunciation of the inadequate Messianic idea of the Pharisees.

It is the absence of this inspiring idea which makes his confessions morally so great a disappointment. A writer may be as severe as he will on the sins and follies of the present, if only he leaves open a door of hope for the future. Carlyle is commonly thought a gloomy writer, but he is a truly edifying one, because on the whole, at any rate in his time of vigour, he believed in progress. Who is not helped morally by that fine passage in *Sartor Resartus?*—

"Generations are as the Days of toilsome Mankind; Death and Birth are the vesper and the matin bells, that summon Mankind to sleep, and to rise refreshed for new advancement."

Contrast this fine but most dispiriting passage in Ecclesiastes:

"One generation goes, another comes,
  But the earth abides for ever;
  The sun rises, and the sun goes down,
  And pants to his place where he rises;
  The wind goes to the south, and whirls about to the
    north,
  Whirling about continually;
  And upon his circuits the wind returns.
  All streams run into the sea, and yet the sea is not full;
  Unto the place whither the streams go, thither they go
    again.

All things are full of weariness ; no man can utter it ;
The eye is not satisfied with seeing, nor the ear filled with
   hearing.
The day that has been is that which will be,
And that which happened is that which will happen,
And there is no new thing under the sun." *

O lame and impotent conclusion! Why, Montaigne can teach us something better than that ; for he declares that "the human spirit is a great worker of miracles." And it is certain that such miracles can only be wrought through the enabling power of that supreme Wisdom who was in the beginning with God, and has "her delight in the race of men," who cannot be hindered, is ready to do good, is kind to man, steadfast, sure, free from care, having all power, overseeing all things.† Such at any rate was the belief of the greater Hebrew sages, and though this noble idea, partly, perhaps, derived from Persia, was now, through Greek influence, lost by a leading writer, it was destined to be brought into fresh prominence at no distant date on the hospitable soil of a Hellenised corner of Egypt.

For some reasons I should be glad to pause here. The exceptional character of the author of Ecclesiastes has a fascination for me, and I would rather that the spell should remain for the present unbroken. But historical fairness compels me, at the

* Eccles. i., 4–9. † Wisd. vii., 22, 23 ; cf. Prov. viii., 22–31.

Orthodox and Heretical Wisdom 209

risk of weakening the effect of the preceding study, to introduce the reader to a less interesting but hardly less important student of wisdom. I refer to the author of Ecclesiasticus. For I must not let you suppose that all the wise men of the later period resembled the unfortunate author of Ecclesiastes, or that heresy had a greater vogue than orthodox wisdom.

The Wisdom of Jesus the Son of Sirach (or Ben Sira, as I shall call him) was probably written about 200 B.C. It is of the religious views of the author that I have now to speak. I shall base my statements as much as possible on the Hebrew portion of the text which has lately been discovered.

And, first, I think we must observe a decided abatement in the cosmopolitan tendency of Hebrew Wisdom. The author of Ecclesiasticus makes frequent reference to Israel, and its spiritual primacy among the nations.* And in the Praise of Wisdom, which, in imitation of Proverbs viii., he feels bound to give, he goes beyond his model in the declaration that, though in all the earth she had a possession, yet her permanent home was in Jerusalem; he even says that she is identical with "the Book of the Covenant, the law which Moses commanded us."†

---

* Ecclus. xvii., 17; xxiv., 8; xxxvi., 12; xxxvii., 25.
† Ecclus. xxiv., 23.

This is a statement which no Alexandrian Jewish scholar would have made, and which has distinctly Zoroastrian affinities, for Dîn or Daêna, the impersonation of the Zoroastrian Law, is called one of the heavenly creations of "the much-knowing Lord," Ahura-mazda.* Later on, it became a fundamental Jewish tenet that the pre-existent, creative Wisdom was no other than the Law.†

Ben Sira, then, honoured the Law, and was impelled to do this more openly than the moral teachers before him. If he does not mention Ezra among the famous men of old, it is simply because the only public services assigned to Ezra by the record were such as it would have equally depressed Ben Sira to speak of, and grieved his disciples to hear.‡ Practically, however, his respect for the Law is tempered by his regard for the other religious classics of his people, from all of which he borrows phrases impartially. That he troubled himself much about ritual details is not probable. It is true, he says that sacrifices, being ordained, are not to be neglected, but he also says that deeds of loving-kindness are the true thank-offerings, and that to forsake unrighteous-

---

* See the Din-Yast, *Zend-Avesta* (Oxford), ii., 264 *ff.*

† Ezr. vii., 25, points in this direction. *Cf.* also the saying of Simeon the Righteous, quoted already.

‡ Even of Nehemiah, Ben Sira can only report that he had restored the walls and set up the gates (Ecclus. xlix., 13).

ness is a propitiation,* and in the temple services it is the external pomp together with the music and singing which attracts and delights him. Doubtless he honours highly the priests, the sons of Aaron, whose privileges he contrasts advantageously with those of the family of David.† This naturally followed from his respect for the Law. But it is as the guardians of the visible centre of the Jewish church-nation, much more than as sacrificers, that he venerates the priests.

The hope of the Messiah is less real to our author than to the older sages,‡ but his doctrine of the latter days is more developed than theirs. Firmly as he believes in present retribution, he cannot do without a final judgment, and that strange prophecy of Malachi, which is even to-day such a power in the Jewish world, respecting the reappearance of the prophet Elijah, is referred to with undoubting belief by Ben Sira. When Elijah comes, the crisis in Israel's fortunes will have arrived. All the other eschatological prophecies will then be realised in blissful experience :

> " Happy is he who sees thee [viz., Elijah], and dies,
> For he will not die, but live indeed." §

---

* Ecclus. xxxv., 1-6.

† Ecclus. xlv., 25 ; David's inheritance was "only from son to son" (so Heb. text).   ‡ See Lecture IV.   § Ecclus. xlviii., 11.

True, Malachi's prophecy by itself does not warrant this, but taken in combination with another great prophecy it does. In the Book of Isaiah we read that, in Mount Zion, God "will annihilate death for ever." * Therefore the righteous whom Elijah finds alive will pass at once into the new life without tasting death; Ben Sira's correction in the second line of a word in the first line has a fine rhetorical effect.

There is no dualism and no pessimism in the author of Ecclesiasticus. "When the wicked man curses Satan," he says, "he curses his own soul,"† for the tempter called Satan is identical with the inborn tempter of the heart—the weak or depraved will. From all troublesome speculation Ben Sira escapes into that picture-gallery of Jehovah's works which we already know from the Book of Job. There is no room here either for an Adversary or for the spectre of Disillusionment. At the conclusion of his summary of the marvels of nature, Ben Sira says, with devout simplicity:

"More in this style we will not add;
  The end of the discourse is, He is all.
  If more were disclosed, we should (still) not search
    Him out,
  For greater is He than all His works.

.   .   .   .   .

* Isa. xxv., 8.   † Ecclus. xxi., 27.

What man has seen Him, that he might tell us?
What man can magnify Him as He is?
There are yet many things that are greater than these;
But little of His works have I seen.
Jehovah has made all that is,
And to His pious ones He has given wisdom." *

I cannot, however, take leave of Ben Sira without comparing him with another writer, who represents a slightly different type of piety. The author and compiler of Chronicles (which, by rights, should include Ezra and Nehemiah) was by calling doubtless one of the Levitical musicians; his date is fifty or sixty years earlier than that of Ben Sira. The man is often more interesting than his work; or rather, the work is often most interesting as a veiled picture of its author. The Chronicler is, of course, more attracted by the details of the ritual than Ben Sira, the layman. It is a pleasure to him to give somewhat minute descriptions of the services and even of the vessels of the temple, nor does he betray any depreciation of animal sacrifices; he could hardly have gone so far towards non-sacrificial religion as Ben Sira and some of the psalmists.

It is obvious that he takes a special interest in those functions of his own class which have no connection with sacrificing. He mentions a Levitical

* Ecclus. xliii., 27-33.

scribe as early as the reign of David, and says that Jehoshaphat sent Levitical teachers of the Law to all the cities of Judah. These were functions which could also be discharged by laymen, and which were destined to overshadow those belonging properly to the priests. Still more interest does he show in the temple psalmody; he assumes as a matter of course that the existing arrangements date back to the tenth century. His interest was fully shared by Ben Sira, as we see from the Praise of Pious Men in Ecclesiasticus. Probably, however, neither of these writers realised the vast spiritual influence of the writers of psalms.

That Ben Sira believes in a present retribution, we have seen already. The Chronicler, however, supplies still stronger evidence of the renewed vitality of this belief in the third century. I need not quote all the astounding distortions and inventions of fact into which the Chronicler's pious illusion has led him. Quite enough has been said against the Chronicler as a historian; let an appreciative word be spoken of the Chronicler as a man. In that age, to believe so earnestly in the justice of God was a service to morality for which we may well condone a score of violations of historical accuracy, and the idealisation of David is as much a prophecy of the better age to come as the vision of the Prince of Peace and the

Rod from Jesse's stock. For eschatological descriptions the Chronicler had no space. But the profuseness with which he deals out imaginary prophets to the earlier ages assures us of his eager desire for a true prophet of the good old style, just as his insistence on the divine justice convinces us that he must have prayed daily for the advent of Israel's true king, Jehovah.

One more point of contact with Ben Sira and still more with the Psalter must in conclusion be mentioned—the tenderness of his piety. I put his theology aside, and speak only of his feeling, as expressed in the speeches which he assigns to his personages. The words in which David blessed Jehovah before all the congregation (1 Chron. xxix., 10–19) may be instanced. They are not indeed such as David could possibly have uttered, but with a few omissions, they might have been used by a pious Levite in leading the devotions of humble-minded Jewish believers. Here, as at other points of his faulty historical reconstruction, the worthy Chronicler opens a window in his heart. And no attainments of intellectual wisdom are worth as much as that loving reverence for God in which he lived and moved.

LECTURE VI.

Judaism : its Power of Attracting Foreigners;
its Higher Theology; its Relation to
Greece, Persia, and Babylon.

IN the third Lecture we studied those exquisite poems on the Servant of Jehovah which represent a perfect fusion of the legal and the prophetic religion. The Servant of Jehovah, *i. e.*, the company of religious teachers which formed the kernel of the Jewish people, was to convert, first, lukewarm or indifferent Jews, and then the other nations to the true religion. The spirit·of his preaching was prophetic; the basis of his message was legal. That Jehovah (interpreted to mean "He who is," *i. e.*, the ground and source of all being and all true knowledge and power) is the God of all mankind, is a belief which underlies the very first section of the Priestly Record (Gen. i.), and how much in earnest the narrator is, appears from the fact that he reports an "everlasting covenant" between the true God on the one hand and mankind represented by Noah and his three sons on the other (Gen. ix., 1-17). It is this "everlasting covenant" which a late prophet declares that the earth's inhabitants have broken,* and which one of the "pillars" of the early Christian community takes as the basis of the new elementary law of Gentile Christianity.† The priestly narrator in Genesis does not, of course, mean that the simple precept of respect for life, and especially for human life, will suffice as the sole constitutional principle of civil society, but he is well assured that the neglect of it will bring the wrath of God upon the offending nations. Does not this throw a fresh light on that otherwise startling statement in the Ninth Psalm ‡:

"The wicked will depart to the nether world—
All the nations that are forgetful of God"?

It is the barbarity of the foreign oppressors of the Jews which forces this bold announcement from the lips of the oppressed. Israel personified knows that God will not allow His command to be transgressed with impunity, more especially when the very existence of His people is imperilled. At another point in the same psalm (Ps. ix., 11, 12), the psalmist shows the intensity of his faith by imagining himself in the happy time when Jehovah will have already interposed. He says:

* Isa. xxiv., 5. † Acts xv., 20. ‡ Ps. ix., 17.

" Sing praise to Jehovah, whose throne is in Zion,
Publish His deeds among the nations,
(Say) that the avenger of bloodshed has been mindful
　　of them
(And) has not forgotten the cry of the sufferers."

We see now that there are supposed to be two classes of persons in the non-Jewish world. There are those who are so "forgetful of God" and His primæval revelation as to touch the very apple of His eye* (viz., the pious community of Israel), and there are those who, though as yet ignorant, are by no means unsusceptible of instruction.† Towards the former class no expressions of hostility seem too strong for some of the psalmists (see Lecture III.), but towards the latter we have the kindest of words from the poet and teacher who wrote the songs on the "Servant." The latter writer had a fellow-worker in that accomplished narrator who, partly on a basis of folk-lore, composed the story of Jonah. Jonah, son of Amittai, was a missionary prophet, who was at first untrue to his vocation, but afterwards went to Nineveh, and sought, not unsuccessfully, to move its bloodthirsty people to repentance. He is intended as a type of the people of Israel, which in the olden time had neglected its missionary calling and as a punishment had been swallowed up by the dragon Babylon, but

---

* Zech. ii., 8. † Isa. xlii., 4.

Judaism

was now liberated, and summoned once more to perform its duty.

A more practicable object, however, than that suggested in Jonah occurred to the mind of another earnestly devout man. It had reference to the foreigners who had begun to be attracted by the religion of Jehovah. These proselytes were above moral or religious reproach; they were zealous in all legal duties known to them, and especially in the observance of the Sabbath. Their chief desire was that expressed so beautifully by a psalmist,*—" to dwell in the house of Jehovah all the days of their life," *i. e.*, to settle at Jerusalem, and to frequent the temple. But they knew only too well the strength of the opposition that was being raised to their request. Their unknown friend sought therefore to help them by a prophecy,† in which God expressly demanded the greatest liberality towards those devout foreigners who were willing to comply with legal requirements, on the ground that His house was to be regarded as the universal house of prayer. Though not richly gifted as a writer, this good and wise man had at any rate a sound religious insight, and the Jewish Church might well be thankful that priests and scribes like Ezra were not its only directors.

* Ps. xxvii., 4. † Isa. lvi., 1-8.

And again the tale-writer supports the prophet. There was at Jerusalem another friend of the oppressed proselyte, who wrote an idyllic story to justify admitting into the community any foreign women who heartily adopted the nationality and religion of their Jewish husbands. On the lovely story of Ruth I could find it in my heart to say much, were it not that a much-respected American scholar * has already placed the book in its true light before American readers. The existence of this undoubtedly post-exilic book is as important a fact as the rigourism of Ezra. It shows that we are right in holding that that great priest and scribe did not gain an at all complete victory over the friends of mixed marriages. Had the intermarriage of Jews and Moabites become as a matter of fact impossible, such a story could not have been written. But though not impossible, the practice was doubtless frowned upon by the orthodox, and our author, who sympathised with oppressed Moabite women, as Malachi sympathised with oppressed Jewesses, devoted his skilful pen to their cause. Nor is this all. A drier writer, with a turn for genealogies, gave this popular tale a short supplement,† the object of which was to introduce the Moabitish heroine among the ancestors of David. I

* Prof. C. A. Briggs, *North American Review*, Jan., 1897
† Ruth iv., 18-22

am sorry that so good a man as the Chronicler did not take the hint. We look in vain in *his* genealogy of David for the name of Ruth. Possibly he was afraid to recognise this supposed Moabitish wife of Boaz, who might be taken to have conveyed a taint to her posterity; for we can hardly doubt that he ascribes the wickedness of King Rehoboam to the Ammonitish extraction of that king's mother.*

The generosity of prophet and tale-writer must not, however, be exaggerated. Whatever pride a foreigner had taken in his birth or riches or wisdom had to be laid aside when he became a proselyte. The only nobility worth having was to be of the Jewish religion, and the best use of riches was to "beautify the place of God's sanctuary, and to make His footstool glorious" †; while, as to wisdom, whatever licence might be allowed to a Jew who had returned to Palestine after a lengthened foreign sojourn, the only temper befitting a proselyte, who had so much to learn before he could be perfect in the Scriptures, was that expressed in the words:

> "Not haughty, Jehovah, is my heart,
> Not lofty are my eyes;
> Neither move I amidst great matters
> And things too arduous for me." ‡

Nor is it likely that there were many proselytes in

* 2 Chron. xii., 13, 14.   † Isa. lx., 13.   ‡ Ps. cxxxi., 1.

Judæa, even when the relations between Persia and the Jews were most friendly, and at a later day the disturbed condition of the Persian Empire must have been adverse to any strong Judaising movement, whether in Palestine or elsewhere. The Jews themselves, too, became more and more bitter towards foreigners, and if the two controversial passages against idolatry inserted by a post-exilic editor in the genuine word of the Second Isaiah* belong to the Persian period, we can hardly wonder if the heathen retained their aversion to Judaism, for the tone is unconciliatory and sarcastic, and there is no positive religious teaching such as might attract thoughtful inquirers. Circumstances were indeed most unfavourable to the missionary ideal of the great "Servant"-songs, though one is thankful to record that in the Fifty-first Psalm pious Israel acknowledges its obligation to teach God's ways to sinners and apostates:

> "Gladden me again with Thy deliverance,
> And uphold me with a zealous spirit.
> Then will I teach apostates Thy ways,
> So that sinners turn back to Thee." †

By "sinners" and "apostates" the psalmist means unfaithful Jews.

* Isa. xliv., 9-20; xlvi., 6-8; *cf.* Ps. cxv., 4-8.
† Ps. li., 12, 13.

It is in the 119th Psalm (a work of the Greek period) that we find the passages most suggestive of missions to the non-Jewish world. They occur in two neighbouring couplets:

"And snatch not the word of truth utterly out of my mouth,
For I wait for Thy judgments."
"And I will speak of Thine admonitions before kings,
And will not be ashamed."*

The former couplet reminds us of the "covenant" in Isaiah lix., 21, according to which the words put into the mouth of the true Israel shall never depart from it, *i. e.*, Israel shall be preserved forever in order to be the faithful preacher of Jehovah's law.† In the latter couplet the speaker (pious Israel personified) may perhaps mean that he will venture as a missionary into the presence of heathen kings, as Jonah is said to have done, and this may have been suggested by some recent attempt to place Judaism in a favourable light before a king of Egypt or Syria. I think myself, however, that a more modest profession is made. Israel expresses its willingness to bear witness to revealed truth before kings under changed circumstances. At present such an heroic venture is impossible. At present Israel is too impatient for

---
* Ps. cxix., 43, 46.
† There is an allusion to the soliloquies of that great typical missionary—the Servant of Jehovah.

judgment to be executed on its persecutors,* and suffers too much from the attempts of heathen teachers to draw away its own members to heathenism, to think seriously of missionary enterprises in heathendom. The most that it can do is to cultivate faith in the perfection of the true religion.

> "I have more insight than all my teachers,
> For Thine admonitions are my meditation."

> "The law of God's mouth is better unto me
> Than thousands of gold and silver." †

We find, however, distinct references to proselytes in two psalms ‡ placed very close to the 119th. An invitation to trust in God, and to declare His loving-kindness, is addressed to three classes of persons, viz., Israel, the house of Aaron, and the fearers of Jehovah. "Israel" is used elsewhere as an expression for the laity; the house of Aaron are the priests; the "fearers of Jehovah" must surely be the proselytes, an identification which has later usage in its favour, and can only be doubted by those who regard Psalms cxv., cxviii., and cxxxv. as works of the Persian period—a very improbable hypothesis.

It may therefore, I think, be assumed that at some time in the Greek period, probably during the rule

---
* Ps. cxix., 84.   † Ps. cxix., 99, 72.   ‡ Ps. cxvi., cxviii.

Judaism

of the Ptolemies, and again after the first victories of the Maccabees, a number of foreigners joined the Palestinian Jewish community. Their motives no doubt were various. There were many who thirsted for "living waters" which no other religion possessed*; the comparative spirituality of Jewish monotheism answered to a want of the age.† There were others, perhaps, who felt still more strongly a desire for some bond of union which would be superior to the disintegrating influences of a crushing, despotic rule. Such a bond the Jewish society with its multiplying branches seemed, and rightly seemed, to furnish.

But the most remarkable of all the testimonies to the presence of foreigners in the no longer merely national Jewish Church are those in the appendix to Isaiah xix. (vv. 18–25) and in Psalm lxxxvii. In both passages the belief is expressed that not only isolated individuals, but whole communities, will enter the Jewish fold. No doubt this was a great illusion, but it implies that numerous conversions had already taken place, and that not only Bashan and Galilee,‡ but cities and districts in the various countries men-

---

* Ps. lxv., 2 : "O Thou that hearest prayer ! to Thee doth all flesh come."

† At an earlier period we find an Ammonite (Tobiah) among the Samaritan worshippers of Jehovah.

‡ *Cf.* Ps. lxviii. 22 (?) ; 1 Macc. v. 14–54.

tioned, had become in an appreciable degree Judaised. I will quote the second passage in a form which approximates, I hope, to the writer's meaning. It is a poem in three stanzas of five lines each.

" Thou hast founded her on the holy mountains !
   Jehovah loves the gates of Zion
   More than all (other) dwellings of Jacob.
   Gloriously will I praise thee,
   Thou city of God !

" Rahab and Babylon I will celebrate as her friends ;
   Behold, Philistia and Tyre,
   With the people of Cush—each of these was born there.
   Jehovah will note in the register of peoples,
   This one (and that one) were born there.

" And Zion each one calls Mother,
   Yea, each one was born therein ;
   And (God) Himself establishes her.
   And (this anthem) will be sung in the congregations,
   All my fountains are in thee."

It is the eulogy of Zion as the metropolis of an ideally catholic church which we have before us. The psalmist has absorbed all the great ideas of the Second Isaiah and the Songs of the Servant, and finds them becoming realised in his own happy experience. Whether by preaching, or simply by letting its light shine, the once despised Israel is now attracting Palestinians, Egyptians, Ethiopians, Babylonians, in such numbers that a day seems com-

Judaism 227

ing when all mankind will be Jews, *i. e.*, when religion will unite more than the accidental differences of language or national character separate. The Second Isaiah seems to anticipate that foreigners will only be able to become Jews by sacrificing their national peculiarities. But our poet, and the author of the appendix to Isaiah xix., clearly anticipate that Egypt and Babylon will remain Egypt and Babylon,* even when their higher life and their truest happiness are derived from Zion.

These two passages (the psalm and the prophecy) represent the high-water mark of religious liberality in Palestine. For a moment it seemed possible that Jewish theology might be purged from its darker elements. But this was not to be. It would lead me too far to inquire into the causes of this impossibility. The time warns me to turn aside to a still more interesting subject, which takes us into the very heart of the higher Jewish theology, and is suggested by that congregational anthem in the Eighty-seventh Psalm, " All my fountains are in thee."

What, I would ask, are the fountains in Zion which attracted so many pious proselytes? The image is a speaking one. Who does not remember the beautiful old Hebrew song in the early history, beginning, " Spring up, O well; sing ye to it," † as if by

---

* See especially Isa. xix., 24, 25. † Num. xxi., 17, 18.

song the water hidden in the ground could be coaxed into appearing? But the water which the gracious Mother Zion gives her children is no ordinary living water. Whosoever drinks of the Abana and the Pharpar will thirst again. But he that drinks from Zion's fountains will never thirst; that precious water will be in him as a well springing up into everlasting life.* Here is a fine passage which expresses these ideas very clearly, and notice how in the first couplet the spiritual privileges referred to are thrown open to all mankind:

"(In Thee) do the race of men (put their trust),
 In the shadow of Thy wings do they find refuge.
 They feast upon the delicacies of Thy house,
 And of the river of Thy pleasures Thou givest them
   their drink.
 For with Thee is the fountain of life;
 By Thy light do we see light." †

The last couplet is also important. It shows that there are two kinds of light and life, and that only in the temple can the higher light and life be obtained. What this meant to the noblest Jews, we shall see later. It is plain that the old phraseology is being stretched to admit new ideas. No doubt we must be careful not to spiritualise too much. The blessings hoped for by pious worship-

---

* See John iv., 13, 14.   † Ps. xxxvi., 8–10.

Judaism 229

pers are still, to a large extent, material. To some extent to all men even now, and still more to those who shall be alive at the great Judgment Day, material prosperity will be granted as the reward of faithful obedience. But the new longing for moral oneness with God as certainly tends to become predominant over the old longing for material happiness.

But let us be more definite. Was there no dawning sense of a second life after the sleep of death—a second life which could be measured by hundreds of years, or even perhaps not be measured at all? Certainly from the close of the Persian period some men began "faintly" to "trust the larger hope." It was at this time that the following strongly contrasting sentences were uttered by a prophetic or apocalyptic writer:

"The dead will not live; the shades will not arise; therefore Thou didst punish, Thou didst destroy them, and madest all their memory to perish." (This refers to the dead oppressors of Israel, who are no longer terrible, because the dead (heathen) cannot live again.) "Thy dead shall arise; they that dwell in the dust shall awake and sing for joy. For thy dew is a dew of lights, and the land shall bring forth the shades." *

This second passage is addressed to Israel, and implies that the belief in a resurrection of pious Jews

* Isa. xxvi., 14, 19.

had already found some acceptance. It even appears that mystical expressions had been coined to symbolise this belief. The Resurrection is ascribed to a dew which descends from that highest heaven, where are those dazzling bright lights amidst which God dwells. It is possible, indeed, that this great boon was limited to those who had died for the faith, but even if this were the case at first, we may assume that the humble confessors of daily life would soon look for the same privilege as the martyrs.

About 170 years later, the belief was restated in still more definite terms. The author of Daniel says that in a time of unparalleled trouble the Jewish people will be delivered, and also that "many of those who sleep in the dust of the ground will awake, some to everlasting life, and some to shame and everlasting abhorrence," and that a reward of special splendour is reserved for the teachers of righteousness.* After this time the evidences of the belief in the Resurrection are abundant, though the Sadducees, like the philosophic author of Ecclesiastes, still held out against this foreign-looking innovation.

There is, however, no early evidence for a belief in conscious communion of the soul with God between

---

* Dan. xii., 1-3.

death and the Resurrection, and it was a long time before the abolition of death for righteous Jews in the Messianic age became a general expectation. The last chapter but one in the Book of Isaiah, which dates from the age of Nehemiah, in a description of Messianic felicity, only states that weeping and lamentation will be no more, and that the youngest man who dies in Jerusalem will reach the age of a hundred.* A little later we find another prophetic writer expressing in choicer language the sure hope of the abolition of sorrow. He calls sorrow "the veil that is spread over all peoples," and adds that "God will wipe away tears from off all faces." † More this pious optimist does not know how to say. But a later writer, whose faith in God is such that he boldly hopes for the most stupendous of boons, has inserted this short passage, which interrupts the context indeed, but must have justified itself to readers by its sweetness: "He will annihilate death for ever." ‡ This is the logical outcome of the faith in the Resurrection, and the Jews, as soon as they saw this, vied with their Zoroastrian brethren in the earnestness with which they accepted it.

We could not, therefore, be surprised if we found in Job, Proverbs, Ecclesiasticus, and the Psalter more or less distinct expression of the new beliefs.

* Isa. lxv., 19, 20.   † Isa. xxv., 7, 8.   ‡ Isa. xxv. 7 (line 1).

For no part of any of these books can be earlier than the age of Nehemiah, and a great part even of the Psalter must be later than this period. Even Ben Sira, however, the devout-minded author of Ecclesiasticus, though he holds theoretically that "that which comes from heaven returns to heaven," * yet, as a practical man, recommends cultivating cheerfulness on the ground that there is "no coming up again" from the grave.†

Turning next to Proverbs, we find that not one of its supposed references to Immortality is trustworthy. The most striking passage, if correctly read, would be this (I quote from the Revised Version):

"In the way of righteousness is life,
And in the pathway thereof there is no death."‡

But there is good reason to believe that the second line should rather be read thus:

"But the way of the abominable leads to death."

The true view of the proverb-writers is that expressed in the couplet:

---

* Ecclus. xl., 11, 12.

† Ecclus. xxxviii., 20, 21. There is, indeed, a passage which states that "those who do things that please the Lord will receive the fruit of the tree of immortality." But this is not found in the best Greek MSS., and forms part of an interpolation.

‡ Prov. xii., 28.

> "The fear of Jehovah prolongs days,
> But the years of the wicked shall be shortened." *

In spite of what is urged in the Book of Job, they believed that religion lengthened life and irreligion shortened it, while the final proof of the moral government of the world would be given at a great crisis (the Messianic Judgment), when destruction would come on the wicked as a whirlwind.† It is true that this attitude of the wise men might conceivably be due to educational reserve. To draw moral arguments from an unverifiable idea of quite recent origin might seem injudicious, as tending to promote a too enthusiastic habit of mind. But nothing can diminish the force of these affecting lines from a speech of Job :

> " For (hope) exists for a tree,
>   (And for a fig-tree there remains) a future ;
>   If it be cut down, it will sprout again,
>   And its shoots will not be wanting.
>
> " But when man dies, he passes away,
>   He breathes his last, and where is he ?
>   Till the heavens wear out, he will not awake,
>   Nor arouse himself out of his sleep." ‡

And even more thrilling is the denial of a second

---

* Prov. x., 27 ; cf. iii., 2, 16 ; ix., 11.
† Prov. i., 27.
‡ Job xiv., 7-12. The first stanza in the received text is probably incomplete.

life which follows, because the speaker admits that he would so gladly think otherwise. There is, in fact, no passage in the whole Bible which more clearly proves the congeniality of the greatest of all hopes, at any rate to Semitic human nature, and of course I need not say that Aryans and Semites on this as on some other points closely resemble each other.

" Oh that Thou wouldst put me in ward in Sheól,
   That Thou wouldst hide me till Thy wrath were spent,
   That Thou wouldst appoint me a time and remember me,
   (And) that a man, though dead, could live again !

" Through my long hard service then would I wait
   Till my relief should come,
   Till Thou shouldst call, and receive my response,
   Till Thou shouldst long after the work of Thy hands.

" But now Thou countest each step that I take,
   Thou wilt not pass over my sin ;
   Thou hast sealed up in the bag my transgression,
   Thou hast secured with wax mine iniquity." *

The beauty of this is that the longing expressed by Job is, I will not say so impersonal, but so unselfish ; he craves to live again in order to enjoy the happiness of conscious communion with God, and would gladly wait in the drear city of Death till the divine call came, if a second life for man were only

* Job xiv., 13-17.

possible. He knows indeed (or thinks that he knows) that the idea lacks foundation, and yet he cannot help luxuriating in it for a moment, for it is so sweet. But it is very significant that he never refers to it again. The supposed reference to the Resurrection in chapter xix. (see Lecture V.) is due partly to corruption of the text, partly to the instinctive belief of the later Jews that so precious a hope must have found a place in the wise old poem of Job. The passage being mutilated, the editor in the simplicity of his heart endeavoured to fill it up in a worthy manner. But what he produced is certainly not worthy of the author of Job as a specimen of Hebrew writing.

This result need not greatly surprise us. Professional students and teachers are afraid of opening the door to religious enthusiasm. But in hymns intended for congregational use a larger hospitality to new beliefs may be expected, especially in the Greek period. To decide whether this expectation is correct, we must not rest satisfied with the form in which the Hebrew Psalter has reached us. Further exegetical progress is only possible as a consequence of a searching revision of the text of the psalms. Such a revision, with the assistance of my predecessors, I have endeavoured to make, and I shall now build on the results which I have reached.

The chief passages which have to be considered occur in Psalms xvi., xvii., xlix., lxxiii. These are of extreme interest, and, as they stand in the received text, convey the impression that the writers had had an intuition of a second life for the individual. More especially, if we take the passages in connection with parallel passages in the Psalms of Solomon and with statements in the Book of Enoch, the reference to a future life seems difficult indeed to controvert.

If, however, we approach these passages in the course of searching textual revision our confidence in this conclusion will be considerably shaken. Take Psalm xlix., for instance. If the text is approximately correct, this psalm is closely parallel to chapters cii. and ciii. of the Book of Enoch.* These passages are a protest against the old Hebrew notion of Sheól, or the nether world, which encourages the party of the wicked rich men in their oppression of the righteous poor. And such a protest we find in the Forty-ninth Psalm, according to the received text. The rich man who hews out for himself a grand sepulchre, considers that he will have a correspondingly grand resting-place in Sheól. Of punishment for his oppression of the poor he does not dream. In life and in death he will be equally the

* *Cf.* Lecture V.

spoiled child of fortune, the heir of all such good things as are to be had. To this the psalmist is made to reply that the wicked rich man is profoundly mistaken. The relative position of his own class and of the righteous poor will be inverted. The rich man will go down to join his fathers in Sheól, but without his pomp, while the poor, upright man will be rescued from the grasp of Sheól, and the company to which he belongs will trample on the graves of the wicked when the dawn of the greatest of days appears.

Plausible as this interpretation is, I am afraid that it is incorrect. Textual criticism shows that the contrast in the foreground is not between the fate of all rich men as individuals and that of all poor men, but between that of all rich men without exception and that of the community of the pious, without special reference to this or that individual. Of the fate of the individual poor man nothing is said.* The community would live on, even though all its present members should die. Spiritual self-forgetfulness is incumbent on a pious Jew; he is absorbed in the welfare of the community to which he belongs; the community will, he is fully persuaded, enjoy

---

* An incidental allusion, may, however be found in v. 10. The "wise" who are expressly said to "die" are of course righteous and presumably poor.

eternal life. These, if I am not mistaken, are the words of the psalmist, or rather of the pious community personified :

> "This is the way to their stumbling,
> And the road to their fall which they run."

With these words the poet begins a new section. He describes how the wicked rich men run heedlessly into the arms of ruin. Then he continues :

> "Like sheep, they sink into Sheól ;
> Death rules them, terrors affright them ;
> They go down straight into the grave,
> Sheól is their mansion for ever.
> (But) surely my soul God will set free,
> For from the hand of Sheól will He take me." *

The Seventy-third Psalm is closely parallel to the Forty-ninth It does not give such a graphic description of the fate of the wicked, but, judging from the received text, it draws the same contrast between the future of individual rich men and individual poor men. The Jewish paraphrase (Targum) actually finds a reference to the Resurrection, and Christian interpreters have, by no means fantastically, found one to a Beatific Vision of God immediately after death. The latter view is especially attractive. The story of Enoch, as we know, was popular in the post-exilic period, and it would be extremely natural,

* Ps. xlix., 14-16.

Judaism

in an age of growing individualism, for pious theists to claim for themselves the privilege of Enoch, who, as the traditional story said, "disappeared, for God had taken him."* The words:

> "Thou wilt guide me according to Thy counsel,
> And afterwards take me to glory," †

seem not unworthy of the poet who says a little later that, though his outward form had wasted away, the believer would still have God for his inalienable portion. And yet this attractive theory, which has survived the attacks of exegetical opponents, has, I fear, to be abandoned on grounds of textual criticism. I will read a translation of the most important verses which I believe to be based on an unassailable text. There is a contrast, as you will see, between the fates of the righteous and of the wicked.

> "How are they [viz., the wicked] brought to desolation in a moment,
> Utterly swept away by terrors (of death)!
> As a dream when one has awaked,
> So, Lord, when Thou art aroused, Thou wilt despise their phantom-like form.
>
> "And yet I am continually with Thee;
> Thou hast taken hold of my right hand:

* Gen. v., 24.
† According to Kautzsch's new (German) translation of the Old Testament.

>   According to Thy counsel Thou wilt guide me,
>   And make known to me the path of glory." *

Who the speaker is, and what the "path of glory" means, I will explain presently. But it must already be clear that the second line of the last couplet is parallel to the first, and that both lines refer to some uniquely great experience upon this material earth.

We now turn to the Seventeenth Psalm, the received text of which permits a reference to a Vision of God after death. Indeed, I may even say that it favours such a reference, for a contrast appears to be drawn † between the speaker, who hopes to see God "at the awaking," and the "men of the world, whose portion is in this life." And yet, a strict textual criticism compels us to abandon this theory. What the psalmist wrote may not be in all points certain. But the following gives, I am sure, no incorrect view of the meaning:

>   "Up, Jehovah, confront him, make him bow down ;
>   Rescue my soul from the wicked, Jehovah !
>   Their portion give unto them—their share of (Thy)
>   wrath ;
>   Fill their body with Thy stored-up punishments !

---

* Ps. lxxiii., 19, 20, 23, 24. The rendering of Wellhausen and Furness in the *Polychrome Bible* is based on a correction which hardly touches the root of the evil.

† So, at any rate, in the English version.

"As for me, in mine innocence I shall behold any face,
I shall feast mine eyes when thy zeal awakes."*

The speaker now becomes, not an individual Israelite, but the Jewish people, over which Jehovah says that He watches as the "apple of His eye." †

One more passage only remains—Psalm xvi., 10, 11. The received text is here quite unobjectionable; it may be translated thus:

"For Thou wilt not yield my soul to the nether world,
Nor wilt Thou suffer Thy pious one to see the pit.
Thou wilt make known to me the path of life;
Before Thy face is abundance of joys,
Delights are in Thy right hand for evermore." ‡

Now it has always been felt that the case for what I may call the mystic interpretation was weaker in this passage than in those which we have been hitherto considering. The phrase "the path of life" in Proverbs § is generally supposed to mean that course of action which leads to a happy life; and certainly "joy before the face of Jehovah," and gifts from His hand, are assigned in Psalm xxi. to an earthly king ‖; while to be delivered from Sheól may merely mean to escape from peril of death.

* Ps. xvii., 13–15.
† Ps. xvii., 8; cf. Deut. xxxii., 11.
‡ Ps. xvi., 10, 11.
§ Prov. ii., 19; v., 5, 6; cf. x., 17.
‖ Ps. xxi., 6.

Hence many critics have supposed the meaning of the passage to be this—that the individual who is taken to be the speaker will be delivered out of his present distress, and recover the blissful consciousness of the divine favour. Others have felt that this view does injustice to the grandeur and solemnity of the passage, and I so fully agree with them that, if the received text of the three other passages were correct, I should not hesitate to find in all four alike a reference to the hope of Immortality. It is no objection to this view that it may involve supposing that the psalmist passes over the death of the righteous, and represents future blessedness as the sequel of present obedience and faith. For if death is merely being received to God's glorious presence, according to the ordinary interpretation of Psalm lxxiii., 24, there is no reason why death should not be passed over, and it is certain that the idea of a foretaste of rewards and punishments prior to the Judgment was familiar to the later Jews. But we have seen that the three other passages, correctly read, do not permit the mystic interpretation, and consistency compels us to give it up for the fourth. This does not, however, involve the acceptance of the favourite critical view just described. For the "path of life," even in Proverbs, is not, I believe, only the course which conduces to happiness, and still less does it mean this in the Sixteenth Psalm. "Path of life" and "path of glory" both refer to the Messianic age, when, as another psalmist says, "glory will abide in our land."* It is the divine glory which is meant, and "life" is not merely what in these dim days we call happiness, but such an intense life as is described in these words of a late prophet:

> "And I will rejoice over Jerusalem, and exult over My people;
> And the sound of weeping shall no more be heard in her, nor the sound of crying.
> They shall not build, and another inhabit; they shall not plant, and another eat:
> For as the days of trees are the days of my people." †

It is true that phrases like those in the last two lines of Psalm xvi. are used in Psalm xxi. of an earthly king. But who is that earthly king? Not any historically known king of Israel, but the expected Messianic king, who is in fact but the leader and representative of the community, so that what is said of him can equally well be said of personified Israel, and even (at least to a great extent) of each pious Israelite. Certainly it is of a pious individual that Jehovah is made to say by a psalmist:

> "I will rescue him and make him glorious;
> I will satisfy him with length of days,
> And grant him to see My deliverance," ‡

---
* Ps. lxxxv., 9.   † Isa. lxv., 19, 22.   ‡ Ps. xci., 15, 16.

where no doubt the blessings intended are those of the ideal or Messianic age.

So, then, in none of the passages quoted, and if not there then certainly nowhere else, does the Psalter contain any reference to the Resurrection or to Immortality for the individual, which shows that down to the time of Simon the Maccabee these closely related beliefs were not held by the majority of the pious. Still they must have been held by an important minority. The ideas were, so to speak, in the air, and they corresponded to religious needs, which were more and more felt, especially during the sharp persecution of Antiochus Epiphanes. We may be sure, therefore, that the glorious but vague expressions of the four passages which have been discussed, and of others which might also be quoted, were very early applied to the individual, and interpreted in what I have called the mystic way. These passages, and not the melancholy couplet:

"What man can live on, and not see death,
  Or win escape for his soul from the hand of Sheól?"*

must have been the spiritual food of the most fervent Palestinian Jews in the Greek period—of those Jews whose successors became the members of the large and important school of the Pharisees and of the sect of the Essenes.

* Ps. lxxxix., 48 (probably, however, an interpolation).

Judaism

And now let us leap over the interval between Simon the Maccabee and the Roman general, Pompey, who put an end to the Asmonæan kingdom, B.C. 63. The belief which was formerly that of a minority has become generally accepted. Between 63 and (say) 45 B.C. eighteen fresh psalms were written and collected, forming the so-called Psalter of Solomon, in which without the least vagueness the Resurrection and Immortality of the righteous are described as certain.* The evidence of this is abundant. We find this saying, for instance: "The life of the righteous is for ever, but sinners shall be taken away into destruction, and their memorial shall no more be found." † And again: "The destruction of the sinner is for ever; but those that fear the Lord shall rise unto eternal life; their life shall be in the light of the Lord, and shall not fail." ‡ There is also one very striking passage in this late Psalter in which pious Israelites are described as "trees of life." They "live for ever," not, as the Book of Enoch says of the elect, by eating ambrosial fruit, but by "walking in the law which God commanded us." § So, too, the Targum of Jonathan (on

---

* Probably the second of the Eighteen Benedictions, which describes God as "He that brings the dead to life," is somewhat older than this period.

† Psalms of Solomon xiii., 9, 10.

‡ *Ib.*, iii., 15, 16. § *Ib.*, xiv., 1, 2; Enoch xxv., 5.

Gen. iii.) represents that the study of the Law is a surer way to Immortality than tasting the fruit of the tree of life, and the appendix to the Sayings of the Fathers* says that the Wisdom which is "a tree of life to those who lay hold on her" (Prov. iii., 18) is—the Law.

Thus the later writers (always excepting such heretics as the author of the original Ecclesiastes) infuse a fuller meaning into the old phraseology. They do so quite simply and as a matter of course, and I confess that their view seems to me to give the worthiest interpretation of the consecrated words. At the same time, I must recognise the fact that the old psalmists themselves meant something different, and express my admiration for these noble thinkers, who, in Browning's language, † were much less sure of soul than of God—for the author of the Seventy-third Psalm, for instance, who says:

"Whom have I (to care) for in heaven?
  And possessing Thee, I have pleasure in nothing upon earth.
  Though my flesh and my heart had wasted away,
  God would be my rock and my portion for ever."

Could you have questioned this psalmist on his theology, you would probably have found him on the side of Antigonus, the Jewish preacher of disin-

---

* *Pirqe Aboth*, vi., 7.   † See *La Saisiaz*.

terested morality, mentioned already. But as you read on, you see that he is on the verge of a fuller intuition. For he continues:

" Surely those that remove from Thee shall perish ;
Thou destroyest all those who wantonly desert Thee.
But as for me, nearness to God is my happiness ;
In the Lord Jehovah I have put my trust." *

To us it may seem as if the promise of the destruction of the wicked were a guarantee of the salvation of the righteous. But this unselfish thinker is content with the present bliss of communion with God, nearness to whom is all the happiness that he personally desires. That Israel will be saved, he cannot doubt. Even if the destroyer could silence the last of God's confessors by the cold steel, the breath of God would breathe upon the dry bones, and they would live. God would still be Israel's rock and its portion forever.

But what *is* " nearness to God," according to early Jewish piety? Ezekiel speaks of the priests, the "sons of Zadok," as alone competent to draw near to God. But the psalmist's experience is one that is not confined to priests, for, as one of the latest psalms says, the pious, collectively, are " the people of those who are near to Him." † From a Judæan point of view, it is in the temple that nearness to God is

* Ps. lxxiii., 27, 28.   † Ps. cxlviii., 14.

chiefly felt, where art and religion combine to lift the humblest believer above himself. How could the daily routine of legal obedience be felt irksome when it was sweetened by a real, even if mystic, vision of God and by the grand psalmody of the temple? The impressiveness of the temple services can be imagined from the descriptions of the Chronicler, and from the glowing words of Ben Sira in Ecclesiasticus. They would not, of course, have commended themselves altogether to our taste, but they were admirably adapted to the people who used them. "How goodly," says one of the psalmists,

"How goodly are the processions of God,
 The processions of my God, my king, in the sanctuary.
 Singers go before, minstrels follow after,
 In the midst are damsels playing on timbrels.
 In a full choir they bless God,
 (Yea) the Lord, the leader of Israel." *

And then turn to the "finale of the spiritual concert" of the Psalter—the 150th Psalm, which I do not quote only because it is among the best known of all the psalms. Certainly the Jews felt music and singing to be what Western Christians are wont to describe as "means of grace."

In an elaborate ritual system like the Jewish there was, of course, great danger of superstition. No

* Ps. lxviii., 24-26.

doubt many Jews thought that their connection with Jehovah could be renewed by a merely mechanical performance of sacred rites. But the best teachers consistently protested against this view. Only a "righteous people" could draw near to God and benefit by the sacramental rites, and by righteousness the psalmists mean, primarily, religious morality. Here is a passage in which the Jewish Church solemnly repudiates all sympathy with the party of the wicked:

"I hate the congregation of evil-doers,
And never sit in the conclave of the wicked;
I wash my hands in innocence,
So will I go (in procession) round Thine altar, Jehovah!
That I may proclaim with loud thanksgiving,
And tell out all Thy wonders." *

We also have in Psalms xv. and xxiv. two poetic church catechisms describing the conditions of admission to the highest of all privileges. The conditions mentioned are moral ones, and the privilege offered is absolute security under the divine protection. A special name for their privilege is Guestship. "Who may be a guest in Thy tent, Jehovah?" † asks the pious community; and at the Messianic Judgment we are told that sinners in Zion will tremblingly ask:

* Ps. xxvi., 5–7. † Ps. xv., 1.

" Who can dwell as a guest beside the devouring fire?
Who can dwell as a guest beside the perpetual burnings?" *

The old conception of guestship was a very different one. The guests of Baal and Astarte were no better than parasites, feasting at the sacrificial meals, but owning no extraordinary moral obligations.† But the guests of Jehovah (the Jehovah of the psalmists) had received from Him a new moral standard, and high as their aim was, always saw perfection above them, for "Thy commandment is exceeding broad." ‡ Now and then the guests of Jehovah might be afraid of being burdensome to Him; they might think they saw a frown upon His face, and remind Him with tears of their Guestship. § But this was in times of more than usual national distress; the normal state of feeling for a "guest of Jehovah" was certainly a joyous one.

The new and purified conception of a guest of Jehovah was one of the greatest religious consequences of the Dispersion of the Jews. It had become impossible to hold that the privilege of Guestship was confined to residents in Jerusalem. Tens of thousands of pious men could only visit Jerusalem once in their lives; many more could never do so at all.

---

* Isa. xxxiii., 14.
† Renan, *Histoire d'Israël*, iii., 35.
‡ Ps. cxix., 96.
§ Ps. xxxix., 12.

And yet they were conscious of no weakening of their connection with Jehovah, because they had begun to learn the secret of spiritual prayer. In their private chamber and in the synagogue a strange new experience had proved to them the loving care of their Protector, radiated, as it were, from Zion to any "dry and thirsty"* corner of God's world where they happened to be. Even if there were a superior efficacy in prayers offered in connection with the temple sacrifices, yet the liturgical services of Zion were for the good of Jehovah's people in all lands. It was even commonly supposed that by simply turning in prayer towards Jerusalem three times a day,† a Jew in Persia or Egypt might obtain the same advantages as a Jew who prayed in the temple. This nascent belief in spiritual prayer certainly influenced the Jews of Jerusalem, many of whom, indeed, must have had occasion when away from home to prove its truth by experience. And thus to the conception of a spiritual Israel, gained from the Second Isaiah, was superadded that of a spiritual temple. To those who, at

* Ps. lxiii., 1.
† Dan. vi., 10; cf. 1 Kings viii., 48. This was a Zoroastrian custom, except of course as regards turning towards Jerusalem. The Zoroastrian precept was, "Three times a day one must worship, standing opposite the sun" (*Pahlavi Texts*, Sacred Books of the East, Part iii.). The first prayer was to be at daybreak. Hence at any rate probably came the Jewish custom of saying the first prayer at dawn. Cf. also Koran, Sur. xvii., 80.

a distance from Jerusalem, read the Twenty-third Psalm, the words:

> "I shall dwell in Jehovah's house
> For all days to come," *

must have acquired a deeper meaning than the poet intended. The temple of which they thought was one which no unfit worshippers could desecrate, and which had a loftier roof and wider courts than could be seen on Zion. Religious patriotism forbade them to express this idea, but in their heart of hearts they very nearly agreed with those words of Browning:

" Why, where's the need of temple, when the walls
O' the world are that ?   What use of swells and falls
From Levites' choir, priests' cries, and trumpet calls ? "

The conception of a spiritual temple naturally leads on to that of spiritual sacrifices. The origin of this conception, which is very plainly expressed in the Psalter, may safely be traced to Jeremiah. This prophet, in opposition to the legalists of his day, emphatically denies that God gave any other directions to the ancient Israelites than this: "Obey My voice, and I will be your God, and ye shall be My people." † As the context shows, he means the

---

* Ps. xxiii., 6.

† Jer. vii., 22, 23 ; Amos had said virtually the same thing (Am. v., 25).

Judaism

moral law. Now there was a school of thinkers in post-exilic times who were of one mind with Jeremiah. Among its earlier members are the authors of Psalm xl. (part 1), Psalm l., and Psalm li., 1-17. It is not necessary to suppose that these writers were as violently opposed as Jeremiah to the sacrificial system; they may very possibly have held that sacrifices were provisionally enjoined for the "hardness of men's hearts." But they certainly held that the only essential statutes were the predominantly moral ones summed up in the Decalogue. I will quote those passages of the Psalms which are most in point. In the first I have been obliged to add a few words to complete the sense.

> " In sacrifice and offering Thou delightest not,
> (But) ears hast Thou created for me.
> Burnt offering and sin-offering Thou requirest not,
> [My heart hast Thou renewed.]
> To perform Thy will,
> O my God, I delight;
> [Thine ordinance] and Thy law
> Are within my heart." *

The closing words remind us once more of Jeremiah, who assures us that in the latter day God will "put His law into Israel's inward parts, and write it in their hearts" †—words which express the highest intuition of pre-exilic prophecy.

* Ps. xl., 6, 8. † Jer. xxxi., 33.

In the next passage those Jews who frequent the temple but break Jehovah's fundamental statutes receive a severe castigation. This is coupled, not with a command to perform the usual rites in a better frame of mind, but with this surprising injunction:

> "Sacrifice to God thanksgiving,
> And pay thy vows to the Most High;
> And invoke Me in the day of trouble:
> I will rescue thee, and thou shalt glorify Me." *

And the closing words of the psalm are:

> "He that sacrifices thanksgiving, glorifies Me,
> And to him that is of blameless life I will show the deliverance of God." †

Here we have not only sacrifices but even vows, which affected daily life still more than sacrifices, abrogated by being spiritualised. The only right vows are vows of amendment of life; the only right sacrifice is thanksgiving for God's innumerable mercies to Israel. The criticism applied by the author of Ecclesiastes (see Lecture V.) to the popular sacrifices and vows of his own time illustrates and justifies the language of the psalmist.

Last of all, listen to these lines from the Fifty-first Psalm:

> "Thou hast no pleasure in sacrifices and offerings;
> In burnt offerings (and whole burnt offerings) Thou delightest not.

* Ps. l., 14, 15.   † Ps. l., 23.

The sacrifices of God are a broken spirit ;
A broken and contrite heart, O God, Thou canst not despise." *

Here we have in germ the doctrine of the later Judaism that repentance is tantamount to burnt offerings. A later writer, however, was dissatisfied with this, and added a rather poor appendix.† He did not deny that God was at present quite indifferent to sacrifices —the misfortunes of Israel too plainly proved this, —but he thought that when the ruined walls of Jerusalem were rebuilt, He would once more be pleased with the "right sacrifices"—a vague expression which seems to mean sacrifices offered, not with the view of changing God's purpose, but out of obedience to His declared will. He belonged, that is, to a theological school which accepted the sacrificial system without criticism as of divine appointment, but gave it a new symbolic meaning. Of this school the author of Isaiah liii., who speaks of the self-oblation of a martyr as a true "offering for sin," seems to have been also a member.

So, then, there were other places besides the temple where God was felt to be near, viz., the private chamber and the synagogue, and those who could only find God here could perfectly well sing the psalm, "Jehovah is my shepherd ; I want for noth-

* Ps. li., 16, 17. † *Ib.*, vv. 18, 19.

ing." Prayers and praises were their sacrifices, and one more service there was which is only not called a sacrifice because it had no connection with the temple—the study of the Scriptures. Did Ezra perceive that he was digging the grave of the sacrificial system when he recognised the principle of a written revelation? At any rate such was the result of the gradual canonisation of the Law, the Prophets, and the Writings; inspired books must necessarily be vehicles of the divine spirit, and to commune with them is equivalent to communing with God. It was in the Greek period (to which the psalms on the Law appear to belong) that this high view of the Scriptures began to be prevalent. The more dangerous Hellenism became, the more the pious Jews sought an antidote to it in their Bible, and after the Maccabæan rising the veneration for the Scriptures became such that "in them" the Jews "thought they had eternal life."* They felt that here was a moral sublimity to which Greece could offer no counterpart, and a bond which could unite the scattered members of their race far more effectually than the temple at Jerusalem. And history justified their conviction. More and more offence was given to all high-minded Jews by the chief ministers of the sanctuary, and when the vengeance of implacable

* John v., 39.

Rome demanded the final destruction of the already desecrated shrine, it was a comfort to the Jews to know that their greatest treasure was saved. The golden candlestick might be carried away by victors, but the sun of the spiritual firmament remained, "and there was nothing hid from the heat thereof." *

How it came to pass that the possession of a sacred volume failed to secure Jewish religion against change, it is not for me to describe. Suffice it to say that the changes which have passed, and which are still passing, over Jewish religious thought are not greater than those which passed over it within the Biblical period. I have found it impossible to give even this brief sketch of post-exilic religion without alluding from time to time to foreign influences. The influence of Greek thought cannot be definitely traced in the early Greek period; we first find it in Ecclesiastes. But the inquisitive spirit which produced that remarkable book doubtless existed earlier; the Book of Job, though Hebraic in forms of expression, represents a new departure in Jewish thought, which cannot be dissociated from Greek influence. Persian influence did not begin to be strongly felt by Palestinian Jews as early as has been supposed. The Ahura-mazda of the Avesta has no doubt a strong affinity to the Jehovah of the later

* Ps. xix., 6.

Jewish writers, but the old attraction to Babylon for a long time prevented this newly discovered affinity from producing much effect. Some effect of course there must have been, but we are not in a position to calculate its amount. Before the arrival of Ezra it was probably almost confined to the large Jewish colonies on the east of the Euphrates and the Tigris, and even in Babylonian-Jewish works like the Priestly Code, in the Cosmogony for instance (where we might have expected something different), it is Babylonian rather than Persian influence which is most clearly traceable. It is true, the conception of the pre-existent heavenly Wisdom in the Prologue of Proverbs has Zoroastrian affinities, and at an earlier date we meet with a belief in a Resurrection, which can hardly have developed without Persian stimulus. But the Prologue of the Book of Proverbs is a work of the early Greek period, when Persian influence can without difficulty be admitted, and the belief in a Resurrection was not (as it would seem) originally accompanied by a belief in Immortality,* though the two beliefs go together in genuine Zoroastrianism.

---

* The two beliefs were combined by the Essenes, if Josephus's account of this sect may be trusted (Jos., *Ant.*, xviii., 1, 5 ; *cf.* xiii., 5, 9). Their doctrine of the soul combines two elements—a Babylonian and a Persian—both Hebraised (Cheyne, *Origin of the Psalter*, p. 419).

The truth is that we cannot sharply distinguish between the two classes of influences—Persian and Babylonian. Ancient Persia and ancient Israel were both influenced by Babylon, and the influence of Babylon upon Persia began probably at a much earlier date than has been supposed. Babylonian deeds show that Persians resided in Babylon before the conquests of Cyrus, and the religion of Ahura-mazda, though more akin to that of Jehovah than to that of Marduk or Merodach, may perfectly well have been influenced, like its Jewish sister, by the latter. I feel sure that it was so influenced, and that those scholars who would explain all Jewish or all Persian ideas from unassisted internal movements are in the wrong. The development both of Jewish and of Persian religion is no doubt for the most part perfectly natural; but the development would not have taken quite the same course but for certain atmospheric influences, if I may use the phrase, which came from Babylonia. Hence it is frequently difficult to offer absolutely convincing proofs of the indebtedness of Judaism or Zoroastrianism to Babylon, and, for a similar reason, of the indebtedness of Judaism to Zoroastrianism. Some obviously direct loans there are, but generally we have to be content with showing the probability of indirect religious influence. This, however, will certainly not be difficult to show to those who have any familiarity with the study of comparative religion. And not to trouble you with further details, I maintain that, as illustrations of the movement of Jewish thought indicated by the Psalter, the ancient Zoroastrian hymns called the Gâthâs* are more instructive than any of the religious utterances in either the earlier or the later Babylonian inscriptions. They are quite as free from superstitious ceremonialism and as uncompromising in their ethical demands† as the Hebrew Psalms, and it can hardly be denied that the communings between God and Zarathustra (who is practically the impersonation of the pious community) can only be equalled in spirituality by the very finest parts of the temple hymn-book.

Such are the historical results which, after divesting them of troublesome technicalities, I have felt moved to lay before you. But before I conclude, let me urge upon you not to let these historical inquiries languish. If there are other voices which sound more enticing to the men and women of this generation, it does not follow that they are really more important than the call to search the Scriptures. Religious reform is a necessary condition of

---

* See *Zend-Avesta*, vol. iii. (Sacred Books of the East).

† The extension of morality to the thoughts ("good thoughts, good words, good deeds") is as characteristic of the Gâthâs as of the Psalms. *Cf.* Ps. xvii., 3-5.

Judaism

social progress, and with a view to this the origin and nature of essential Christianity, and—shall I add?—of essential Judaism, has to be investigated afresh. Deeply as it stirs our feelings, none of us should refuse to take his part in this grave debate. I do not undervalue the study of the early Israelitish religion; indeed, I could wish to have included its records within my survey. But it is the study of the religious formation which developed out of this which has the most claim on our attention, because of its close relation to the historical problems of early Christianity. It is itself not without its thorny regions, but amidst the thorns we are surprised by delightful blooms, the efflorescence of the religious spirit of Judaism. I have done what I could within the necessary limits to dispose some of these flowerets to the best advantage. If the Songs of the Servant of Jehovah, the composite Poem of Job, the Psalter, the Books of Wisdom, the narratives, at least, of Ezra's law-book, and the narrative of the Chronicler have in some of their aspects become more living realities to my readers, I shall feel that my visit to America, which has now become a treasured memory, was not altogether useless.

INDEX.

Agur, sceptical poet, 174 ff.
Angel of repentance, 18
Antigonus of Soco, saying of, 190, 198, 246
Artaxerxes, why favourable to the Jews, 38
Atonement, Day of, 75
Augustine of Canterbury, 27
Aurelius, M., 194
Azazel, 76

Babylonian, influences, 130, 259; kings, 107
Behemoth and Leviathan, 154 n.
Bernard, St., 190
Bickell on Ecclesiastes, 184 f.
Bildad, influence on Job's development, 168
Branch, origin of Messianic title, 15
Briggs, Dr. C. A., 220
Browning, 246, 252
Buddhism, ideal king of, 101

Cambyses and Egyptian religion, 41
Carlyle, quoted, 207
Chaos unknown to Job, 154
Chronicler, piety of, 215; Levitical interest, 213 f.; attitude towards ritual, 213; attitude towards Gentiles, 221; as an historian, 197, 214
Church, Jewish Catholic, 226 f.
Congregation, the, 62–64
Cosmogony, Babylonian affinities of, 258
Creation, new conception of, 154

Cyrus, policy of, 82

David, symbolic use of, 96

Ecclesiastes, a "Song of Songs" (?), 183; unity questioned, 183 f.; how made orthodox, 184; cool theism of, 186; attitude towards the Law, 189; attitude towards immortality, 191; attitude towards marriage, 191 f.; Stoic affinities of, 198; character of author, 191, 194 f., 205 ff.; date of, 197 ff.
Ecclesiasticus, its devout simplicity, 212; attitude towards wisdom, 209; attitude towards the Law, 210 f.; attitude towards future life, 232; attitude towards Messiah-belief, 211; attitude towards nature, 212; date of, 199, 209
Egyptian, priest, a parallel to Nehemiah, 40–43; religion, 60
Elihu, speeches of, 18, 171
Elisha ben Abuyah, a sceptic, 178
Emerson, quoted, 155
Enoch, 151, 155, 158 f., 177 n., 181, 239; Book of, 151, 155, 176, 181, 203 f., 236
Essenes, 200, 203 f., 244, 258 n.
Ezekiel, influence of, 24 f., 165
Ezra and Nehemiah, historicity of, 56

Index

Ezra, his character and career, 59, 69 f.; object of his migration, 54; his supposed firman, 55 f., 70 f.; his attempted marriage reforms, 56-62; his relation to the congregation, 62-64; was he a priest? 55
Ezra's lawbook, not at once generally accepted, 57 f., 62; not merely legal, 77; not altogether his work, 72; in what sense new, 72 f.

Fasting, 9-11
Fatherhood, the divine, 59, 60
Frazer, author of *Golden Bough*, 75

Gentiles, Jewish attitude towards, 134, 218 ff.
Gerizim, Mt., temple on, 28, 32 f.
Geshem, the Arabian, 45
God, names of, 175; dual aspect of, 166-168; sons of, 175 f.
Goethe, quoted, 174
Greek thought, 158, 173, 178, 196 f., 206, 257
Guests of Jehovah, idea of, 250

Haggai, 8 f., 11-13
Handel, his *Messiah*, 99
Haupt, Professor, 5, 185
"Heads" of the Jewish community, 6, 10, 16
Herod the Great, 200
Holiness, ceremonial, 74
Hooker, quoted, 154
Hope, the larger, 229
Humility, 80
Hyrcanus, John, 199

Ideals, Jewish religious, 82 ff.
Immortality, 229-244
Inspiration, Book of Wisdom on, 133; Philo on, 133

Jannæus, Alexander, 199

Jeremiah, anti-sacrificial school of, 252 f.
Jeshua, high priest, 6
Jews, three classes of, 125; number of, in the community, 65 n.; why so few returned at first, 21
Job, a poetical version of Abraham, 79; original Book of, 160 ff.; early legend of, 159 ff.; and his friends, rôles transposed, 165 f.; of Edomitish origin (?), 132; insertions in Book of, 171 ff.; and the Servant of Jehovah passages, 162; on future life, 17, 23 f., 63
Jonah, story of, 91, 218
Josephus, cited, 39, 200, 258

"Kiss the Son," a misunderstanding, 112
Koheleth, *see* Preacher
Koran, cited, 251 n.

Loeb, on the Psalms, 113

Maccabee, Simon the, 244
Macdonald, Prof. D. B., 160
Manasseh, Jewish priest, 32, 68
Messiah, the, 94 ff., 243
Milton, quoted, 144
Mommsen, quoted, 4
Montaigne, 183, 208
Mountain, the divine, 110

Nathan, prophecy of, 109
Nature, contemplation of, 172 ff.
Nehemiah, character of, 43 ff.; career of, 37-54, 64-69

Orthodoxy, an early protest of, 179

Pascal, a Hebrew, 164
Paul, St., 59; Pauline theology, 77
Persian influences, 257 ff.
Peters, Dr. J. P., 16 n.

Index

Pharisees and Sadducees, 200, 204 ff., 244
Pirqe Aboth, quoted, 246
Pompey, 245
Prayer, discovery of, 251
Preacher, the, identified with Solomon, 184, 197
Prophets, their activity at Babylon, 21 f.
Proselytes, 219, 221, 224 f.
Proverbs, Book of, an ethical handbook, 173, 208 ; Book of, secular element in, 138 ; Book of, religion of, 139 ff.
Psalter, an historical authority, 124 ; text needs revision, 235 ; twice refers to an historical ruler, 105 ; religious influence of, 74, 204 ; of Solomon, 205, 245

Religion, individual, 166
Religions, historical study of, 261
Renan, his date for Ecclesiastes, 199 ; quoted, 250
Resurrection, 244 ; limitation of, 230
Retribution, doctrine of, 163 f., 211, 214
Rhys-Davids, Professor, 101
Rig Veda, quoted, 178
Ruth, story of, 220

Sabbath, 66 f.
Sacrifices, spiritual, 252-255
Samaritans, the, 25-35, 60, 68
Sanballat, 31, 45, 47, 48, 68
Satan, 18, 212

Scepticism, Jewish, 173, 195 ff.
Servant of Jehovah, 69, 86 ff., 223 n.; songs of, when inserted in 2 Isaiah, 92 ; in Psalter, 93
Sheshbazzar, 6
Simeon, the Righteous, saying of, 190, 210 n.
Sirach, Jesus son of, 209 (*see* Ecclesiasticus)
Solomon, in legend, 128 f., 197
Stanley, Dean, on Nehemiah, 44

Talmud, cited, 201 n., 246
Targum, on Deut. xxxiii., 11, 199 n.; on Psalm lxxiii., 238 ; free treatment of Ecclesiastes, 188 ; on Gen. iii., 245
Temple, spiritual, 251 f., 255
Thutmes III., of Egypt, 110
Tobiah the Ammonite, 45, 65

Virgil, a prophet, 103 n.
Vows, scruples respecting, 189, 254

Wisdom, conception of, 126 ff., 153-156, 159, 176, 209 f., 258

Zechariah, 11-19; his disillusionment, 16
Zend-Avesta, cited, 157, 210, 260
Zerubbabel, 6, 8, 14-16
Zion, meaning of, in 2 Isaiah, 63
Zoroastrianism, 74, 81, 151, 157, 210, 251 n., 258 ff.

BIBLICAL PASSAGES.

1. OLD TESTAMENT AND APOCRYPHA.

GENESIS.

i. 216
ii. . . . . 177 n.
v., 21-24. 155
— 24. 239
ix., 1-17. 217
xviii., 17-19 130

LEVITICUS.

xi., 44. 80

NUMBERS.

xi., 29; xvi., 3. 91
xv., 32-36. 66
xxi., 17, 18. 227
xxiii., xxiv. . . . . 131 n.

DEUTERONOMY.

iv., 10. 130
— 19. 86 n.
vi., 7, 20 $f\!f$. 130
xi., 19. 130
xxxii., 11. 241

JUDGES.

ix., 8-15. 131

RUTH.

iv., 18-22. 220

2 SAMUEL.

xiv., 2. 131
— 17, 20. 131
xvi., 23. 131

1 KINGS.

iii., 28. 131
iv., 29-34. 129
viii., 48. 251

2 KINGS.

xxii., 8. 71

1 CHRONICLES.

xxix., 10-19. 215

2 CHRONICLES.

xii., 13 f. 221

EZRA.

v. 15
vii., 6-10. 71
— 11-26. 55
— 25. 210
— 27 f. 54
ix., x. . . . . 58 f.

NEHEMIAH.

vi., 7. 16
viii. 57 f.
xii., 15-22. 66
xiii., 23-27; 28-30 68

JOB.

v., 12 f. 138
xi., 12. 136
xiv., 7-12. 233
— 13-17. 234
xv., 4 f. 117
— 5. 138

Biblical Passages

JOB (CONTINUED).

xv., 7 f.	149 n., 177
xvi., 18–21	167
xix., 21 f.	168
— 25–29	169, 235
xxi.	79
xxiii., 8	169
xxviii.	171
— 20–23	153
— 26 f.	150
— 28	153
xxix.–xxxi.	170
xxxiii., 23 f.	18
xxxviii.–xli.	171
xxxviii., 22–27	152
— 29–34	152

PSALMS.

i., 2	126
ii.	111, 112
v., 9	120
ix., 11, 12, 17	218
x., 3	119
xii., 1	122
xv.	249
— 5	122
xvi.	241–244
— 1–5	30
xvii.	240, 241
— 3–5	260
xviii.	110, 111
xix., 6	257
xx., xxi.	106
xxi., 6	241
xxii.	93
— 7, 8	120
xxiii., 6	252
xxiv.	249
xxvi., 5	124
— 5–7	249
— 9 f.	123
xxvii., 4	219
— 12	121
xxxi., 18	120
xxxv., 4–6	143
— 11	121
xxxvi., 1–3	116
— 8–10	228

PSALMS (CONTINUED).

xxxvii., 26	122
xxxix., 12	250
xl. (part 1)	253
— 6–8	253
xlii., 3, 4	119
— 4	114
xliv., 24	144
xlv.	106 f., 147
— 4	80
xlix.	236–238
l.	253
— 14 f., 23	254
li., 1–17	253–255
— 12 f.	222
— 16 f.	255
— 18 f.	255
lii., 1	123
lv., 11	122
lxiii., 1	251
lxv., 2	225
lxviii., 22	225
— 24–26	248
lxix., 20 f	118
lxxii.	108, 147
lxxiii.	164, 238–240
— 25, 26	246
— 27, 28	247
lxxxv., 9	243
lxxxvii.	225 f.
lxxxix.	109 f.
— 48	244
xci., 15 f.	243
xcii., 7 f.	143
xciv., 10	135
xcvii., 1–6	111
ci.	105
cx.	105
cxv.	224
— 4–8	222
cxviii.	224
cxix., 43, 46	223
— 72, 99	224
— 84	224
— 96	250
cxx., 2	122
cxxiii., 3 f.	118
cxxvii., 3	24

PSALMS (CONTINUED).

cxxxi., 1 221
cxxxii., 11 96
cxxxv. 224
cxxxix., 21 124
— 24 125
cxliv., 1-11 111
cl 248

PROVERBS.

i., 4 138
— 6 129
— 27 233
ii., 19 241
iii., 2, 16 233
— 14-16 138
— 18 246
v., 5 *f.* 241
viii., 4 134
— 5-12 138
— 18 *f.* 138
— 22-31 .... 149, 208
— 25 .... 177 n.
— 31 134
ix., 11 233
x., 17 241
— 23 136
— 27 .... 139, 233
— 29 139
xi., 30 137
xii., 28 232
xiv., 2, 31 140
— 35 145
xv., 3, 11 140
— 8 141
— 33 139
xvi., 3 141
— 4 .... 143, 153
— 7 142
— 10 145
xvii., 27 138
xix., 17 194
xx., 28 146
xxi., 3, 27 141
xxii., 3 138
xxiv., 11 193
— 17 141
— 21 *f.* 146

PROVERBS (CONTINUED).

xxv., 4 *f.* 146
— 21 *f.* 142
xxviii., 3 123
xxix., 13 144
— 18 145
xxx., 2-4 173-181
— 5-9 180
— 29-31 146
xxxi., 1-9 146
xxxiii., 13-15 140

ECCLESIASTES.

i., 4-9 .... 207 *f.*
— 12-14 198
— 14 *f.* 193
ii., 18 *f.* 194
iii., 11 198
— 21 191
v., 4, 6 188
— 7 191
vii., 2 *f.* 192
— 15 187
— 16 *f.* 188
— 27 *f.* 192
viii., 2-4 202
— 9 192
— 14 187
ix., 2 203
x., 7 .... 201 *f.*
— 16a, 17a 201
— 20 201
xi., 10a ; xii., 1a 192
xii., 11 *f.* 182
— 13 *f.* 197

ISAIAH.

i. 26 102
iii., 4 }
v., 11 } .... 201 n.
ix., 2-7 .... 94, 97, 98-101
xi., 1-8 .... 94, 97, 101-104
xix., 18-25 225
— 24 *f.* 227
xxiv., 5 217
xxv., 7 *f.* 212, 231
xxvi., 14-19 229
xxx., 2 131

Biblical Passages

ISAIAH (CONTINUED).

xxxi., 2	130 f.
xxxiii., 14	250
xl., 13 f.	156
xlii., 1-4	89
— 4	218
— 6	92
xliv., 9-20 } xlvi., 6-8 }	222
xlix., 1-6	88 f.
l., 4-9	88
li., 7-10 } lii., 12 }	24
— 13-15	91
— 13 ; liii., 12	162
liii., 2-9	83
— 10 f.	162
— 12	96
liv., 1	24
— 13	91
lv., 1 f.	23
— 3-5	97
lvi., 1-8	219
— 2-6	67
lvii., 1	85
lviii., 5	116
— 13	67
lix., 20	63
— 21	223
lx., 13	221
lxi., 1-3 } lxii., 1, 6, 7 }	92
lxv., 1 f.	27
— 3-5, 11	29
— 19 f.	231
— 19-22	243
lxvi., 1 f.	28
— 3 f.	29

JEREMIAH.

vii., 22 f.	252
viii., 8	131
ix., 17	131 n.
xxiii., 5 f.	95
xxxi., 33	253
xxxiii., 14-16	95
xli., 5	26
xlix., 7	132

EZEKIEL.

xiv., 14	159
xvii., 22-24 } xxxiv., 23 f. } xxxvii., 24 f. }	94
xxviii., 3	155
— 13 f.	110
xlv., 10-20	75
xlviii., 35	95 n.

DANIEL.

vi., 10	251
xii., 1-3	230
— 3	125

AMOS.

iii., 6	98
— 7	12
v., 25	252 n.
ix., 11 f.	100

MICAH.

iii., 3	121
vi., 8	91

HAGGAI.

ii., 6 f. } — 21-23 }	13

ZECHARIAH.

ii., 8	218
iii., 8 } vi., 12 }	15
v., 5-11	18
vi., 9-12	15
vii., 1-5	10
ix., 9	80, 108
xii., 8	103
— 10	85 n.

MALACHI.

i., 11	28, 133
ii., 8	32
— 10 f.	28
— 10-16	60
iii., 16	20, 63
iv., 1-4	19
— 5 f.	211

ECCLESIASTICUS.

i., 15	134
xvii., 17	209
xviii., 13	135
xxi., 27	212
xxiv., 8, 23 } xxxvi., 12 } xxxvii., 25 }	209
xxxii., 15	127
xxxv., 1-6	211
xxxvi., 1-17	147
xxxviii., 20 *f.* } xl., 11 *f.* }	232
xxxix., 4, 10	134
xliii., 27-33	212 *f.*
xlv., 25	211
xlvii., 17	129
xlviii., 11	211
xlix., 13	210

WISDOM OF SOLOMON.

vii., 22 *f.* 298

2 ESDRAS.

xiv., 44 71

1 MACCABEES.

v., 14-54 225

II. NEW TESTAMENT.

MATTHEW.

xi., 14	47
— 29 *f.*	80 n.

JOHN.

iv., 13 *f.*	228
v., 17	154
— 39	256

ACTS.

xv., 20 217

2 CORINTHIANS.

iii., 2 92

www.ingramcontent.com/pod-product-compliance
Lightning Source LLC
Chambersburg PA
CBHW031334230426
43670CB00006B/340